M000192232

Edith Scholl, ocso

Words for the Journey

A Monastic Vocabulary

MONASTIC WISDOM SERIES
Patrick Hart, ocso, General Editor

Advisory Board

MONASTIC WISDOM SERIES: NUMBER TWENTY-ONE

Words for the Journey

A Monastic Vocabulary

by
Edith Scholl, ocso

Foreword by
David N. Bell

α

Cistercian Publications
www.cistercianpublications.org

LITURGICAL PRESS
Collegeville, Minnesota
www.litpress.org

A Cistercian Publications title published by Liturgical Press

Cistercian Publications
Editorial Offices
Abbey of Gethsemani
3642 Monks Road
Trappist, Kentucky 40051
www.cistercianpublications.org

1	2	3	4	5	6	7	8	9

Library of Congress Cataloging-in-Publication Data

Scholl, Edith.
    Words for the journey : a monastic vocabulary / Edith Scholl ; foreword by David N. Bell.
        p. cm. — (Monastic wisdom series ; no. 21)
        ISBN 978-0-87907-021-2 (pbk.)
        1. Catholic Church—Terminology.   2. Theology—Terminology.
    3. Latin language—Church Latin—Terms and phrases.   I. Title.
    II. Series.

BX841.S36 2009
255—dc22   2009013885

CONTENTS

FOREWORD

David N. Bell

Lung.pa re.re skad.lugs re/
bLama re.re chos.lugs re//

It is perhaps unusual to begin the preface to a book dealing
with Cistercian theology, spirituality, and practice with a quotation in Tibetan, much less one that is not translated. Yet there is
a method to my madness, and those who have tried to pronounce
or mispronounce the sentences (Tibetan pronunciation is as
wicked as English) may be interested to learn that it is—or used
to be—a well-known Tibetan proverb. It means "To each region
its own dialect; to each monk (*lama*[1]) his own doctrine." Two
important points arise from this. First, that unless one knows the
language, it is impossible to translate the saying. And secondly,
that the *chos.lugs*—pronounced something like *chö-luk*[2]—of any
monk or lama is essentially his, or, in the case of Tibetan nuns,
her own. The reason why it is his or her own is simple: language.
The Tibetan Buddhist Canon was, to a large extent, translated
from Sanskrit, and the technical terms in both languages are
replete with multiple layers of meaning. Sometimes those meanings are not the same in both languages, and one person will
interpret a term in one way, another person in another.

We have just the same problem in English. According to the
Christian Scriptures, one of the key commandments is to love

---

1. The initial b of the Tibetan word *bLama* is not pronounced.
2. The *k* at the end is hardly pronounced.

one's neighbor. But what does this mean? The only word on which one might agree is "your," but when we come to "love" and "neighbor" we are in deep trouble. What is love, and who is my neighbor? If the injunction bids us leap the fence between my house and that of, let us say, an attractive woman who lives next door, pounce on her unsuspectingly, and rape her on the spot, then I clearly have a problem. If, on the other hand, it means that I first check to see that my neighbors are good Christians, and then wave to them and wish them well on a Sunday morning on their way to church, I also have a problem. "Love" and "neighbor" are terms of unqualified richness, and we must remember that when Jesus of Nazareth was asked by a certain lawyer, "Who is my neighbor?" he cheated. He did not answer the lawyer directly, but spoke a parable (Luke 10:25-37), and parables are subject to even more levels of interpretation than the terms we are investigating. On the other hand, the saving grace of the commandment comes in the two words at the end. It does not enjoin us simply to love our neighbor, but to love our neighbor *as ourself* (Matt 19:19 and parallels). But that, alas!, simply makes the commandment even more problematical. How and in what way and to what extent should we "love"—whatever that means—ourself? A reader might be more at home in Tibetan.

Other terms are just as difficult. "*What is Truth*, said jesting Pilate, and would not stay for an answer."[3] Personally, I do not think he was jesting, but wanted a clear and straightforward response. If he had asked Jesus of Nazareth "What are facts?" Jesus would have had little problem in replying. That St John's is the capital of Newfoundland and Labrador is a fact. That a hundred cents make a dollar is a fact. But truth and facts, though overlapping, are not the same thing, any more than *veritas* and *factum* (or, indeed, *res*) are synonyms in Latin.

Those who wish to study non-Christian religions are faced with just the same problem. All religions, without exception, are

---

3. Francis Bacon, *The Essayes or Counsels Civill and Morall* (1625), Essay I, the first sentence.

replete with technical terms which, if they can be translated into English at all, can be translated only in a gravely limited way. Three examples will suffice: *dharma* in Hinduism and Buddhism, *dao* in Confucianism and Daoism, and *fanā* in Muslim mysticism. It is perfectly possible to translate these terms as "rule," "way," and "annihilation," but in all cases one barely scratches the surface of what the term really signifies. Indeed, the scratching of the surface itself can sometimes be grossly misleading.

To come closer to home, the same is true of a huge number of words in the Christian Scriptures. Saint John tells us that in the beginning was the Word (John 1:1). But "the Word"—*ho Logos* in Greek—had a richness of connotation, Jewish, Stoic, and Platonic, which is lost in translation and lost to most of us today. The same is true when Saint Paul speaks of "faith"—*pistis* in Greek—or when Saint John, once again, tells us that God is light (1 John 1:5). What sort of light? Does he mean sunlight, electric light, glow-worm light, the light of a candle, all of these, or something quite different? Does he mean, perhaps, *uncreated* Light, different entirely in quality from any created Light, and—as uncreated—participating in the very nature of God himself? Those Eastern Christian mystics known as hesychasts certainly thought so, and their entire spiritual technique was centered upon experiencing in their own soul the uncreated light of God,[4] which, when all was said and done, was a direct participation in the nature of God himself. They did not experience the *essence* of God—God as He is in himself, *sicuti est* (1 John 3:2)—but they did experience God in his manifestations, his *energies*; and just as my little finger is truly part of me, yet not all of me, so the Light of God is part of God, a true experience of God, though not an experience of all of God, which is more than our mortal natures can bear.

It follows, therefore, that in matters of religion and spirituality—and spirituality is no more than religion in practice—the

---

4. The matter is explained in more detail in David N. Bell, *Many Mansions: An Introduction to the Development and Diversity of Medieval Theology, West and East*, (Kalamazoo, MI: Spencer, 1996), chap. IX, 173–91.

simplest phrases can be the most misleading. Or, if not misleading, misunderstood. There is no doubt that this is true of the Cistercian tradition, which is the especial subject of this book. Take, for example, a saying which few who read these words will appreciate, since it comes from one whom most Cistercians love to hate, and who, among many Cistercians, is known only by means of a doctrine of ignorance. I mean Armand-Jean de Rancé, abbot of la Trappe from 1664 to his death in 1700. In a quite wonderful letter, Rancé, speaking of penitence or penance—the same word in French—says that discernment, when free from all laxity and every fleshly indulgence, is a greater virtue than penitence.[5] This is not what many would expect from the abbot of la Trappe, especially those who have never read his works and who, therefore, are better qualified than those who have to express an opinion. Indeed, they might expect him to say that penance or penitence is more important than anything at all. But the key to the statement consists of five technical terms in seventeenth-century French: *discrétion, relâchement, condescendance charnelle, vertu,* and *pénitence.* Without a clear and deep understanding of these terms, we can gain but a clouded and shallow understanding of what Rancé is actually saying. It is not for nothing that discernment— *discretio* in Latin—was called "the mother of the virtues," and those who wish for proof of this point may read it for themselves in Chapter Two of this present book. In this matter, Rancé, as in so many things, is at one with Saint Bernard of Clairvaux.

The same is true of the technical vocabulary of the earlier Cistercian Fathers, those writing in Latin and not the vernacular. Indeed, there are single terms on which whole books have been written, and two examples alone must suffice. What do we mean, and how do we poor unfortunates, we harmless drudges,[6] who try to translate their works, render into English *affectus* and *caritas*?

5. Armand-Jean de Rancé, Letter 75/2; *Abbé de Rancé: Correspondance*, ed. Alban J. Krailsheimer, vol. 1 (Paris, 1993), 664.

6. See Samuel Johnson's definition of a "Lexicographer" in his famous dictionary.

And just to make things worse, what on earth do we do with *affectus caritatis*? Just a few years ago, in 2005, Damien Boquet wrote an excellent study, almost four hundred pages long, on *L'Ordre de l'affect au Moyen Âge*,[7] and he was primarily concerned with only one writer, Aelred of Rievaulx. And if we were to begin listing the books on *caritas*, we would be here for as long as *caritas* itself.

It is precisely here that Sr. Edith Scholl has come to our rescue. That it is but a partial rescue is clear, for her investigations into word after word can have no end, and some of the words will not be fully understood until we have passed beyond the narrow confines of this world and stand upon a wider shore. Yet in this invaluable compilation, we find discussion of *voluntas, discretio, meditatio, quies, misericordia, devotio, pietas, sponte,* the spiritual senses, *dulcedo, excessus mentis* and *raptus,* and—a fitting ending—*fruitio Dei.* All these terms can be translated into English simply and misleadingly by one or two words. But if *pietas* is no more the "piety," in the way that we use the word today, then we have not even begun to scratch the surface of the richness of the term in twelfth-century Cistercian writers, or, indeed, of those in seventeenth-century France, who spoke of *piété* in a way utterly alien to most of us in a twenty-first-century Anglophone or Francophone world.

What the studies of Sr. Edith make clear is that, when we try to read the writings of the great Cistercian *spirituels,* what we read is a sort of spiritual shorthand. Or, if one prefers, they are written in a language whose apparent meaning may sometimes appear obvious, but whose depths go on forever. After all, if we are talking about finding God, whether in himself or ourselves, then we are talking about finding a being who is infinite. The mortal mind, however, is decidedly finite, and our knowledge of God can never, therefore, have an end. "Veil after veil will lift—but there must be / Veil upon veil behind."[8] Indeed, even

---

7. Damien Boquet, *L'Ordre de l'affect au Moyen Âge. Autour de l'anthropologie affective d'Aelred de Rievaulx* (Caën, 2005).

8. Edwin Arnold, *The Light of Asia,* first published 1879, Book VIII.

the most profound mystical experience can only be a progress, an investigation, not a conclusion, and much the same is true of the writings of the great Cistercian spiritual teachers—or, indeed, of the great spiritual teachers of every tradition. As Sherlock Holmes said, "There is as much sense in Hafiz as in Horace, and as much knowledge of the world."[9]

Sister Edith restricts herself to the Cistercian authors of the twelfth century, but there is more to the Cistercian tradition than that. There is as much sense in Rancé as in Bernard, and perhaps an even greater knowledge of the world. Some would say that Bernard transcends his times as Rancé does not, but that is arguable. Both were very much men of their age, and much that has been written of Bernard in recent years is no more than a caricature of the real man. Personally, I would argue that Rancé, who knew and loved Bernard's writings,[10] understood his character better and more accurately than many scholars and devotees of the twentieth and twenty-first centuries. It is all a matter of perspective. We must know where we are, whence we come, and whither we go, and how we perceive a person or an event, and how we express that perception, can only be affected by our time and our place. *Tempora mutantur, nos et mutamur in illis.*

The experience of such perspective is the purpose, or, at least, one of the purposes of *lectio divina*, "spiritual reading." When a monk or nun reads the Scriptures or the writings of any enlightened being, he or she does not read for information, but for transformation. This is the meaning of *ruminatio*, as Sr. Edith makes clear in her third chapter. But she is discreet, she is delicate, she bows her head to our modern sensibilities. What is the real essence of *ruminatio*? Only if we become like bipedal cows can we appreciate it. When it comes to the Word, we should chew it thoroughly and then gulp it down; regurgitate it, chew it over

9. Arthur Conan Doyle, "A Case of Identity," the last sentence. Hafiz is the Persian poet and mystic Muḥammad Shamsuddīn Ḥāfiẓ, who died in 1389.

10. See David N. Bell, *Understanding Rancé: The Spirituality of the Abbot of La Trappe in Context* (Kalamazoo, MI: Cistercian Publications, 2005), 133–36.

again (this is the nasty bit), and gulp it down again; regurgitate it yet again, and again, and again; and only when we have absorbed the entire essence of it can we pass the dross out of our backsides. The spiritual path is harder to follow than a lifetime of back-breaking physical labor. Any Christian worth his or her salt must be a stumbling-block to the Jews and a folly to the Gentiles (1 Cor 1:23), but no one ever said that Christianity was an easy path to follow.

So how do we follow this path? Sister Edith's guidebook provides us with some invaluable keys. She offers us "Words for the Journey." We are *curva* and must become *recta*. We must subsume our *voluntas propria* in *voluntas communis*. If we are images of God, we are flawed images, and our likeness to our Creator (but not the image) has been lost. How do we regain the lost likeness? By using *discretio* which, as we have seen, is the mother of the virtues, and by showing *misericordia* to all who need it. And let us not forget that God will forgive us our trespasses only if we forgive those who trespass against us. It is an awesome responsibility. And what do we have to guide us? *Meditatio* on the word of God, which was not revealed to Christians alone, much less to Cistercians alone, but to all those who, knowing or unknowing, hear the word of the Father in Heaven and keep it (Luke 11:28). But to hear God's word, in whatever language, we must cultivate *quies*—the Orthodox East has much more to say on this than the West—and we must learn to respond *sponte* to the voice of the Holy Spirit.

But listening to the voice of the Holy Spirit is a most dangerous undertaking. Long ago, in the fourth century, a certain council, the first Ecumenical Council held at Nicaea (now Iznik in Turkey) in 325, condemned a certain theological idea. This idea, which had a long previous history, maintained that the Trinity was a hierarchy: the Father was at the top of the Trinitarian tree, the Son was subordinate to the Father, and the Holy Spirit subordinate to the Son. The heresy was linked with the ideas of a fourth-century presbyter of Alexandria called Arius, and is therefore known as Arianism. The Council was right to condemn it,

and rightly condemned it has remained for some seventeen centuries. Yet Arianism is, in fact, alive and well, especially with
regard to the person of the Holy Spirit. Even those who are prepared to admit that Father and Son are equal in all things are
sometimes in doubt as to the Holy Spirit. What, after all, do we
have here? Fathers and sons are well known—we have only to
look around us to see too many of them—but who or what is the
Holy Spirit, and in what way does he, she, or it come into being?
For some churches, the power of the Holy Spirit enables them to
dominate serpents; for others, it demands that they speak in
tongues. But the Holy Spirit is more than this. If we are to believe
the doctrines set forth at the Second Ecumenical Council, the
Council of Constantinople held in 381, the Holy Spirit is wholly
God. To be indwelt by the Holy Spirit, therefore, is to be indwelt
by him who created the worlds from nothing, in whose hands
the Big Bang was but the flicker of a firefly's tail, whose ministers
are flaming fire, and at whose breath the worlds crumble. For too
many of us, the presence of the Holy Spirit is no more than a nice
hot-water bottle on a cold night, a comfortable electric blanket,
but the reality, alas, is very different. The Holy Spirit is a consuming fire, the whirlwind of the will of God, a tidal wave of transformation, containing within itself the serried ranks of the angels,
and the whole power and terror of the tremendous Trinity. If you
listen to *this* voice, you may never be the same again.

But let us go back to the words we quoted earlier: *curva,
recta, voluntas propria, voluntas communis, discretio, misericordia,*
and so on. Some who read this may feel they are indeed reading
Tibetan: the words are not here translated and their meaning is
obscure. If we are *curva*, it is simply the consequence of osteo-
arthritis, and to become *recta* we need only take the appropriate
drugs. This is not quite the case, and Sr. Edith's studies will show
us why it is not quite the case. In this book we find the essence,
or part of the essence, of many of the key terms of Cistercian
spirituality; and since all spiritualities share certain basic funda-
mentals—it cannot be otherwise, given our nature as human
beings—what she says is often generally as well as specifically

applicable. But this leads us to an important point. There is not just one Cistercian spirituality; there are many. That they overlap is not in doubt, but the fact remains that the spirituality of Bernard of Clairvaux was not the spirituality of William of Saint-Thierry; and the spirituality of William of Saint-Thierry was not the spirituality of Aelred of Rievaulx; and the spirituality of Ælred of Rievaulx was certainly not the spirituality of that neglected master, Isaac of Stella. Four lamas, four doctrines (*chos. lugs*). And, if we may take it a stage further, the spirituality of the twelfth-century Cistercians was not the spirituality of such thirteenth-century scholastics as Jean de Mirecourt, Guy de l'Aumône, Jean de Limoges (well worth reading), Jean de Weerde, Humbert de Prully, and Jacques Fournier, who would become Pope Benedict XII. And the spirituality of Jean de Mirecourt was certainly not that of Armand-Jean de Rancé. There are some temptations, says Jean de Mirecourt, which are so great that only a miracle can enable us to overcome them; and if that miracle does not occur, and if we succumb, then we are not in sin. Rancé would not agree.

Yet just as we can take a dozen building blocks and make out of them either a mosque or a monastery, so the basic building blocks remain constant. Our will (*voluntas*) remains our will. Stillness (*quies*) remains stillness, whether we call it *quies* or, in Greek, *hesychia*. Rumination (*ruminatio*)—chewing things over, again and again—remains rumination; and so on. The pages which follow well describe these building blocks, and what use we make of them is up to us. But where do they lead? Here we must be a little cautious.

Sister Edith ends her series of studies with *excessus mentis* and *fruitio Dei*: ecstasy and our fulfillment in God. That Bernard of Clairvaux experienced ecstatic rapture is not in doubt. So did others. William of Saint-Thierry, that Carthusian *manqué*, certainly did, and wrote about it at length, especially in the pages of the *Letter to the Brethren of Mont-Dieu* (the *Golden Letter*)—a work, it must be remembered, not addressed to Cistercians. But we hear little about it in the writings of Jean de Mirecourt and his thirteenth-century confrères, and less in the works of the Great Reformer, the abbot of la Trappe. In a biography of Rancé published in 1814, Charles Butler observed, justly, that prayer at la Trappe

> was both continual and fervent; but it never savoured of refinement, and, in all the agiography [*sic*] of La Trappe, a single instance of mystical excess, or even of mystical prayer, is not recorded.[11] . . . Far from endeavouring to penetrate the cloud with Moses, or to be admitted into the cellar of the Great King (such are the expressions of mystical writers), the monk of La Trappe aimed at no more, than to offer his prayer with the humble publican in the lowest part of the temple, or to fall, with the prodigal, at the feet of his offended but merciful father.[12]

Butler is perfectly correct. Nowhere in his great work, *De la sainteté et des devoirs de la vie monastique*, first published in 1683, does Rancé expostulate on mystical rapture. Not at all. The work of the monk or nun is simple and straightforward: to follow Christ. Indeed, for any Christian *imitatio Christi*, the imitation of Christ, is the beginning and end of the path, and, for a Christian, to imitate Christ is to imitate God himself.

What place, then, does the monastic way hold in this everlasting quest? The answer is simple. The monastery is the equivalent of total immersion when learning a language. Tibetan, with which we began this chapter, can be learned in two ways: from books (and for those interested, there are, these days, many useful guides), or by being parachuted into a monoglot Tibetan village near Lhasa (if such still exists, given Chinese incursions) and expected to fend for oneself. There is no doubt that total immersion was the view

---

11. This is not quite true. There are one or two very rare examples, and Rancé both recognized and acknowledged the reality of extraordinary graces.

12. Charles Butler, *The Lives of Dom Armand-Jean Le Bouthillier de Rancé, Abbot Regular and Reformer of the Monastery of La Trappe; and of Thomas Kempis, the Reputed Author of `The Imitation of Christ'. With Some Account of the Principal Religious and Military Orders of the Roman Catholic Church* (London, 1814), 63–64.

of Bernard of Clairvaux, and there is no doubt that it was also the view of the abbot of la Trappe. Nowadays, admittedly, the situation is a little different—the monks and nuns of the twenty-first century are not the monks and nuns of twelfth- or seventeenth-century France, and things have changed. Yet the essence remains. The monastery is no more and no less than an intensification of everyday life. It is truly a microcosm, and in a microcosm things are concentrated, consolidated, and condensed.

Few are clearer on this point than Baldwin of Forde, later archbishop of Canterbury, a twelfth-century spiritual guide whose solid commonsense and down-to-earth spirituality does not always endear him to modern-day seekers. Baldwin has virtually nothing to say about *excessus mentis*, hardly any words about *raptus*, but he has a very great deal to say about loving one's God and loving one's neighbor, and if one thing is eminently clear, it is that one cannot love the former without loving the latter. Since God himself needs nothing, Baldwin tells us, he has put in his place our brothers and sisters and neighbors who *do* have needs. It is they—images of God—who stand in the place of God. If, then, we do not love our neighbor whom we do see, who stands in God's place, how shall we love God whom we do not see, who does not reveal his presence to us, and who has no needs?

> How else can we offer benefits to God, except by offering them to those in whom God does have a need, who in himself needs nothing? It is God who, in his members, asks and receives; [it is He] who is loved and despised. In the love of our neighbour, therefore, as in the link of love and the bond of peace, we maintain and preserve in ourselves the love (*caritas*) of God and unity of spirit.[13]

But what does it mean to love one's neighbor? We have already mentioned some of the problems, but here we may look for aid to John Henry Cardinal Newman, though we must, of course, make allowance for his Victorian English:

13. Baldwin of Forde, *Sermo* 15.65-66; *Corpus Christianorum Continuatio Mediaevalis* 99 (1991), 245.

It is obviously impossible to love all men in any strict and true sense. What is meant by loving all men, is, to feel well-disposed to all men, to be ready to assist them, and to act towards those who come in our way, as if we loved them. We cannot love those about whom we know nothing; except indeed we view them in Christ, as the objects of His Atonement, that is, rather in faith than in love. And love, besides, is a habit, and cannot be obtained without actual *practice*, which on so large a scale is impossible.[14]

Love, therefore, or, more precisely, that love which is *caritas*, begins at home, with our friends, our fellows, our coworkers, our sisters and brothers in the monastery, our cats, dogs, birds, fish, trees, flowers, and stones. For let us make no bones about it, when God gave this world into our care and keeping, he did not restrict that care and keeping to bipedal hominids. Newman could not have been more correct when he said that love depended on *practice* (his italics), and, save, perhaps, in the greatest of the saints, a lifetime of practice will not suffice for us to love God and our neighbor as God has loved us. So let us not be too hasty to step forth into that "unknown region, where neither ground is for the feet nor any path to follow."[15] Our business is more down to earth.

The monastery is no more and no less than a unique school of love, a *schola caritatis*—the phrase is that of William of Saint-Thierry[16]—and so too is the world. The only difference is that the monastery is a school of total immersion where there is no hiding-place, no concealment. The world, a wondrous miracle of its divine Creator, offers all the same opportunities, yet they are there more scattered, more diffused, more dispersed, and much easier to avoid.

The chapters of Sister Edith's collection show us where we need to go. Where else to start but with the will? With no will,

14. John Henry Newman, *Parochial and Plain Sermons*, ii.54-55, quoted in Erich Przywara, *A Newman Synthesis* (New York, 1945), 248–49.
15. Walt Whitman, "Darest Thou Now, O Soul."
16. William of Saint-Thierry, *De natura et dignitate amoris*, §26.

there is no way; and without a way, we are wandering in the dark. And when we say will, we mean free will. Our will might have been warped and deformed by the first sin, however it be interpreted, but it did not lose its freedom altogether. Augustine of Hippo was quite wrong when he condemned the entire human race as *una massa peccati*, "one lump of sin."[17] We are not, and on this matter, as on others, Saint Augustine was talking nonsense. That we have made a hideous hash of things is not in doubt, but we are not one hundred percent corrupt, and we do not inherit Original Guilt. Augustine has much to answer for. But the use of our human free-will, that sure reflection of our creation in the image of God (few perceived that better than Bernard of Clairvaux), must be tempered with discernment, and only by the use of that discernment can we ponder the word and God, and the Word of God, and not be entirely led astray. And how do we ponder that word?

First, we must learn to quiet our agitated minds—go to the hesychasts for guidance here—and if we cannot do that, then let us ask for help. "Prayer," said Newman, "is the very essence of all religion,"[18] and if he was not quite correct in this matter (and he was not), then his statement remains true for the Christian tradition at least. Indeed, it is the greatest blasphemy to think that we can make our way through this life without divine assistance. It is also stupid. God is there to help us. As the Qur'an tells us, again and again, he is *ar-Raḥmān, ar-Raḥīm*, "the Merciful, the Compassionate," and if he offers us his mercy, which is inseparable from his help, then we are fools not to take advantage of his offer. He will not leave us comfortless. And so it goes on. From mercy to devotion, from devotion to the experience of God, and, in the fullness of time, from the experience of God here on earth to the enjoyment of God in a different state and another plane of being.

17. Augustine of Hippo, *De diversis quaestionibus ad Simplicianum*, I, *quaest.* 2 *argumentum*, and §16.

18. John Henry Newman, *Certain Difficulties felt by Anglicans in Catholic Teaching Considered*, ii.68, in Przywara, 242.

Whether we are granted an *excessus mentis* on the path is
irrelevant. Indeed, it is none of our business. If God decides to
grant it, he will; if he does not, he will not, and that is all there is
to it. Bernard might have been what we may call a "natural mystic," and the same is true of Simeon the New Theologian and a
few others. It was not true of Rancé, and it is not true of most of
us. But the Cistercian way is not a quest for spiritual "highs," or
altered states of consciousness. When the lawyer asked Jesus of
Nazareth what he should do to attain eternal life, Jesus did not
tell him to sit cross-legged on the floor, contemplate his navel,
and seek to rise above himself into that pseudo-Dionysian daz-
zling darkness which so beguiles so many of us today. On the
contrary. What was his reply? "Love God, and love your neighbor
as yourself" (Luke 10:27). It is enough.

Sister Edith's book, therefore, may be of interest or it may
be of use. If it is of interest, it will be rather like reading a "Teach
Yourself How to Drive," while sitting in an armchair and lacking
a car. Entertaining, perhaps, but unproductive. The armchair
does not go anywhere, and by the end of the book one is still
sitting in exactly the same place as one was at the beginning. If
the book is to be of use, it demands work, effort, stubborn bloody-
mindedness, dedication, blood, tears, toil, and sweat. Saint John
of the Ladder, echoing Saint James, put the matter in a nutshell:
"Reading must lead you to action, for you are a doer."[19]

That, indeed, is what is taught and what is offered by all great
spiritual teachers, though they may use strange vehicles for their
teaching. When the great ninth-century Muslim mystic, Abūʾl-
Ḥusayn Aḥmad ibn Muḥammad an-Nūrī, was asked by one of
his pupils where he learned the secret of his absolute *quies*, his
utter stillness in meditation, he replied: "I learned it from a cat at
a mouse-hole: yet he was more still than I."[20] All creation is God's

19. John of the Ladder (John Climacus), *Klimax* (*Scala Paradisi*), 27.78, echoing James 1.22.
20. Farīduʾd-Dīn ʿAṭṭār, *The Tadhkiratuʾl-Awliya of Muḥammad ibn Ibrāhīm
Farīduʾd-Dīn ʿAṭṭār* (London, 1907), vol. 2, 52 (in Persian).

handiwork, and we would do well to heed Saint Bernard when he tells us that we will find more in woods than in books, and that trees and stones will teach us what we cannot learn from professors.[21] The trees and stones are also words for the journey.

Sister Edith, however, has provided us with a book, and a very sensible book it is. The words she offers us to experience are truly words for the journey, though like any journey, they are not without risk. Offering our human will to God is an extraordinarily risky business, for we may rest assured that our prayers will be answered. The problem (for us) is that what we will receive will not be what we want, but what we need, and the two are often utterly dissimilar. As we have seen, invoking the Holy Spirit is a risky business, for he, she, or it, may come as a consuming fire, and it is a fearful thing to fall into the hands of the living God (Heb 10:31). Aslan, after all, is not a *tame* lion. And as for heeding the injunction of all the great spiritual teachers, viz., to know ourselves,[22] that may be the most risky thing of all. To know ourselves, as William of Saint-Thierry and so many others make perfectly clear, is to know both our God-given grandeur and our utter misery. It is to know what we could be, and what we could make of this world (of which we are stewards), and what we have actually made of ourselves and the world in which we live. But all I can say to that is to quote the words of the tenth-century Muslim mystic, Muḥammad ibn ʿAbdi'l-Jabbār al-Niffarī: "In taking a risk, there is part of salvation."[23]

---

21. Bernard of Clairvaux, *Ep.* 106.2.

22. See Pierre P. Courcelle, *Connais-toi toi-même: de Socrate à saint Bernard* (Paris, 1974) (three volumes).

23. *The Mawāqif and Mukhātabāt of Muḥammad ibn ʿAbdi'l-Jabbār al-Niffarī*, ed. and trans. Arthur J. Arberry (London, 1935; repr. 1978), 7, of the Arabic text, the sixth *mawqif*. "Salvation" (*najāh*) can also be translated as rescue, deliverance, redemption, or safety.

INTRODUCTION

In the fifty-eighth chapter of his *Rule*, Saint Benedict directs that newcomers to the monastic life be told all the rugged and arduous ways by which the journey to God is made. The first Cistercian authors—Bernard of Clairvaux, William of Saint-Thierry, Ælred of Rievaulx, Guerric of Igny, Isaac of Stella, Gilbert of Hoyland, John and Baldwin of Forde, Gertrud of Helfta—knew these ways well, as well as the dangers and pitfalls of the journey, but they also knew the joys scattered along the way. They knew too that the journey is not only *to* God, but *with* God, in and through the Christ who called himself the Way (John 14:6). Above all, they never lost sight of the journey's goal: eternal life in the kingdom of heaven. For it was a journey they themselves were making. They had been taught by those who had made the journey before them, and in their writings they transmitted this knowledge, enriched by their own experience, to future generations.

When I started reading and studying these authors years ago, I was struck by their rich vocabulary of Latin words, more or less technical terms, words rich with resonances from Scripture, the liturgy, and patristic and earlier monastic authors: words for which no exact equivalents exist in English.[1] It seemed to me that these words could be a key to a deeper understanding of their message. So gradually I began to dream an impossible dream: a work that would do for these words something of what

---

1. Interestingly, in recent years, the Latin term *lectio divina* has become current, and "affect," a transcription of *affectus*, is also widely used.

Gerhard Kittel's *Theological Dictionary of the New Testament* does for biblical terms, giving each word a range of definitions and sources, observing its development up to the time of Cîteaux, and then, preeminently, its meaning and use in the works of the early Cistercians. Such a work, I hoped, could serve as a companion to the translations being published in the Cistercian Fathers Series, enabling non-specialists to read those translations with greater understanding and appreciation. In fact, it might prove a fruitful source for approaching the whole monastic ethos.

My original list ran to over three hundred words.[2] I soon realized that this was overly ambitious! However, over the ensuing years, I have researched a number of words, and completed twelve articles, eleven of which have been published in *Cistercian Studies Quarterly*, and one in *American Benedictine Review*. From time to time, readers have told me that these articles are helpful. Although I have not given up my research, and hope to produce further studies in the years ahead, it seemed to me that there was enough material already to be assembled in one volume.

Although each article is complete in itself, it does seem that they may be arranged in some sort of sequence, regarding them as stages on the journey to God that, as the Cistercians see it, is a reforming of our original uprightness and likeness to God. The journey begins with turning our wills from our own self-centeredness to God's loving will (*A Will and Two Ways*). A basic virtue, needed at all stages of the journey, but perhaps especially in the beginning, is discretion (*The Mother of Virtues*). Meditation (*Pondering the Word*) and *Stillness* are means to grow in the knowledge and love of God, and most necessary is a deep awareness of both our misery and God's mercy (*Mercy within Mercy*). As we make progress, we act less from constraint and more from *devotio*. It becomes almost second nature to consent to whatever God asks (*Consensus*); our wills spontaneously embrace his (*Spontaneity*). Our spiritual senses develop (*Sensing God; The Sweetness of*

2. See CSQ 27:1, 90–92.

the Lord) and we are taken beyond ourselves (*Going beyond One-self*); we find our *Delight in the Lord*.

I am grateful to everyone who has encouraged me to pursue this project, and in a special way to Dr. Marsha Dutton and Dr. David Bell, without whose support and practical advice it would never have gotten off the ground. The successive editors of *Cistercian Studies Quarterly* have been most helpful. Above all, I want to thank Mother Agnes Day, my abbess for twenty-two years, and my community for their unfailing love all along my own journey, and for allowing me time for research and writing.

ABBREVIATIONS

ACW   Ancient Christian Writers

ANF   Ante-Nicene Fathers

CCCM   *Corpus Christianorum Continuatio Mediaevalis*

CCSL   *Corpus Christianorum Series Latinum*

CF   Cistercian Fathers Series

Conf   *Confessions of Saint Augustine*, trans. Maria Boulding (Hyde Park, NY: New City, 1997)

CS   Cistercian Studies Series

CSQ   *Cistercian Studies Quarterly*

DSp   *Dictionnaire de Spiritualité*

FC   Fathers of the Church

Gray   *The Homilies of Saint Gregory the Great on the Book of the Prophet Ezechiel*, tr. Theodosia Gray (Etna, CA: Center for Traditionalist Orthodox Studies, 1990)

Letters   *The Letters of Saint Bernard*, trans. Bruno Scott James (London: Burns Oates, 1953)

Luddy   *Saint Bernard's Sermons for the Seasons and Principal Festivals of the Year*, trans. Ailbe Luddy, 3 volumes (Dublin: Brown and Nolan, 1923)

NPF   Nicene and Post-Nicene Fathers

Psalms   *Expositions on the Psalms*, Saint Augustine, trans. Maria Boulding, 6 volumes (Hyde Park NY: New City, 2000–4)

Ramsey   *The Conferences of Cassian*, trans. Boniface Ramsey (NY/Mahwah, NJ: Paulist, 1997)

Sermons   *Sermons of Saint Augustine*, trans. Edmund Hill, 11 volumes (Hyde Park, NY: New City, 1990–7)

Chapter 1

A WILL AND TWO WAYS

Voluntas Propria, Voluntas Communis[1]

Where there's a will, the saying goes, there's a way. Christian tradition would rather say that where there is a will, the human faculty of free choice, there is the possibility of two diametrically opposed ways, two contradictory modes of directing one's will— and that the way one chooses to go is of crucial importance. Since it is the wrong way, *voluntas propria*, that receives the most attention in the tradition, we will look at it first.

When used in the pejorative sense, *voluntas propria* is not an easy term to translate or to explain. It is often translated "self-will," but this translation is apt to be misleading. It comes closer to what Gerald May calls "willfulness" and describes as "the setting of oneself apart from the fundamental essence of life in an attempt to master, direct, control, or otherwise manipulate existence."[2] This description is not so different from Saint Bernard's: "By self-will I mean a will that is not common to us with God and our fellow human beings, but exclusively our own: when we will whatever we will, not for the glory of God or the profit of our neighbor, but solely for our own sake."[3]

Having a will of one's own is certainly a good thing, a necessary part of being human. As Saint Augustine points out, the precepts of the law would not be given to us unless we possessed

1. Many of the references for this article were supplied by Irénée Rigolot of the Abbey of N.-D. de Timadeuc, to whom I wish to express my gratitude. See Coll 54 (1993): 356.
2. Gerald May, *Will and Spirit* (San Francisco: Harper and Row, 1982), 6.
3. Res 3.3; Luddy 2:201-2.

1

wills of our own whereby to obey God's commandments.[4] "It is certainly the freedom of the will that is being cited whenever someone is told, 'Be not overcome by evil' (Rom 12:21). For to be willing or unwilling has to do with each one's will."[5] Grace does not deprive us of our free will.[6] "Indeed, when one does [an act] of one's own free will, then it deserves to be called a good work and one for which we are to expect a reward."[7] Saint Bernard declares: "A person's will alone would not be capable of gaining him salvation, but he would never stand a chance of gaining it without his will."[8] It is the will that is saved.

Yet the will is created with the possibility of opposing itself to God's will, with disastrous results, as Augustine emphasizes. "Nothing enslaves the spirit to passion except *propria voluntas* and free will."[9] Sin is to be imputed to the *voluntas propria* of the one who commits the fault.[10]

The experience of evil, Augustine teaches, takes place when one prefers one's own will to the divine will and suffers the consequences of that choice:

> It is impossible for the will of a person not to come tumbling down on him with a thunderous and devastating crash if he so exalts it as to prefer it to that of the One who is his superior.[11]

For Saint Gregory the Great as well, sin is an effect of the misuse of *voluntas propria*.[12] Elsewhere, he speaks of *appetitus*

---

4. Grat et lib arb 4.8; FC 59:259.

5. Grat et lib arb 3.5; FC 59:257.

6. Grat et lib arb 5.2; FC 59:264.

7. Grat et lib arb 2.4, FC 59:255; Gen ad litt 11:21, ACW 42:153.

8. Gra 9; SBOp 3:191; CF 19:92.

9. Augustine, Grat et lib arb 1, 11, 21. (My translation.)

10. Augustine, Gen ad litt 8.14; ACW 42:53.

11. Gen ad litt 8.14; ACW 42:53.

12. Gregory the Great, Mo 9.21.10, CCSL 143:479-80; Mo 15.26.17; CCSL 143A: 767-8.

proprius,[13] *amor proprius,*[14] *arbitrum proprium.*[15] Bernard, for his part, says that "when we are bad we are rightly punished, since we have become so of our own free choice."[16]

It is especially in the monastic tradition that *voluntas propria* becomes a technical term, and the renunciation of it, the fundamental ascetical practice. Some of the sayings of the Desert Fathers illustrate their teaching:

> Abba Poemen said: "The will of man is a brazen wall between him and God and a stone of stumbling. When a man renounces it, he is also saying to himself, 'By my God, I can leap over the wall' (Ps 17:29). If a man's will is in line with what is right, then he can really labor."[17]

> The demons do not fight against us as long as we are doing our own will. Our own wills become the devils, and it is these that attack us in order that we may fulfill them.[18]

> To throw yourself before God, not to measure your progress, to leave behind all self-will, these are the instruments for the work of the soul.[19]

No saying better illustrates the Desert Fathers' attitude towards *voluntas propria* than this quotation: "If you see a young monk climbing up to heaven by his own will, catch him by the foot and pull him down to earth: it is not good for him."[20]

John Cassian expands on the advantages to be gained by renouncing one's will; for one thing, no quarrels arise between

---

13. Reg past 1.7; ACW 11:34.
14. Reg past 2.8; ACW 11:74.
15. Ir 6.35; CCSL 144:570-1.
16. Gra 18; CF 19:74.
17. CS 59:146.
18. *Western Asceticism,* ed. and trans. Owen Chadwick (Philadelphia: Westminster, 1958), 118.
19. Abba Poemen; CS 59:145.
20. PL 73:932.

those who follow not their own will.[21] He may have had in mind that delightful story from the desert:

> There were two old men living together in one cell, and never had there risen even the paltriest contention between them. So the one said to the other, "Let us have one quarrel the way other men do." But the other said, "I do not know how one makes a quarrel." The first said, "Look, I set a tile between us and say, 'That is mine,' and do thou say, 'It is not thine, it is mine.' And thence arises contention and squabble." So they set a tile between them, and the first one said, "That is mine," and the second made reply, "I hope that is mine." And the first said, "It is not thine: it is mine." To which the second made answer, "If it is thine, take it." After which they could find no way of quarreling.[22]

"What effort, or what hard command," Cassian asks, "Can disturb the peace of one who has no will of his own?"[23] Those who withdraw from their own likes and desires, and whose will depends on the will of the abbot, practice the best kind of mortification, a "glorious and valuable violence," and take the kingdom of heaven by force (Matt 11:12).[24]

Voluntas propria is often linked to *concupiscentia*, "the unruly corporal appetite that stands in opposition to the law of God and in which sin reigns."[25] This connection is based on Sirach 18:30: "Go not after your lusts, but turn away from your own will," and Galatians 5:16-18: "Walk in the spirit, and you will not fulfill the lusts of the flesh . . . . [The spirit and the flesh] are contrary to one another, so that you do not the thing that you would." Cassian, as he describes the life of the Egyptian monks, gives this explanation of why the elder's "anxiety and the chief part of his

21. Conl 16.6.4-5; Ramsey 561.

22. *De vitis patrum* 3.96; *The Desert Fathers*, trans. Helen Waddell (1936: Ann Arbor: Ann Arbor Paperbacks, 1957), 142.

23. Conl 24.23; Ramsey 843.

24. Conl 24.26.12; Ramsey 850.

25. Adalbert de Vogüé, *The Rule of the Master*, trans. Luke Eberle, CS 6:43.

instruction . . . will be to teach [the novice] first to conquer his own wishes"; a monk "cannot bridle the desire of his concupiscence unless he has first learnt by obedience to mortify his wishes."[26] Both the Master and Saint Benedict join these two admonitions: "Do not gratify the promptings of the flesh; hate the urgings of self-will" (RM 3.65-66; RB 4.59-60).

The Master comes close to identifying *voluntas proprium* and *concupiscentia*:

> Because all self-will is carnal and issues from the body, its seductiveness leads us to commit what is wrong, and during the short span of this life it seems to the flesh sweet through its desires, only to be more bitter than gall afterwards and forever. Therefore it is right that our tongue should be under compulsion to cry out daily to the Lord: "Your will be done" (Matt 6:10).[27]

Yet the Master also mentions the good results of renouncing self-will:

> Whatever harm the persuasion of the ancient serpent has done us is removed, if we so will, for the will of the Lord heals us. As the apostle says: "You do not always carry out your good intentions" (Gal 5:17) . . . . We therefore pray that the will of the Lord will be done in us. If this his will is always done in us, on the day of judgment there will be no self-will to be condemned.[28]

> [Here on earth] the Lord . . . gives his grace without delay to those who ask for it, shows himself to those who seek him, opens to those who knock. These three gifts granted by the Lord are deserved by those who desire to do God's will, not their own.[29] And those who follow the Lord now will say in the other world, "'We have passed through fire

26. *Institutes* 4.8; NPF 11:221.
27. RM 90.51-54; CS 6:263-4.
28. RM Thp 26-30; CS 6:97.
29. RM 1.74-80; CS 6:110.

and water, and you have led us into a place of rest' (Ps
65:12), that is, 'We have passed through the bitter thwarting
of our own will, and by serving in holy obedience we have
come to the refreshment of your fatherly love.'"[30]

Saint Benedict manifests a profound understanding of *voluntas propria* when, at the beginning of his *Rule*, he addresses
himself to those who are renouncing their own wills (RB Prol. 3).
The word he uses, *abrenuntians*, is not in the Vulgate (Luke 14:33
uses *renuntiat*). It is likely that Benedict is alluding to Cassian's
third conference, *De tribus abrenuntiationibus*, "On the Three Renunciations." The first of these is the exterior renunciation of
home, family, and property. The second is the renunciation of all
the tendencies within us that are opposed to love as Saint Paul
describes in 1 Corinthians 13: anger, jealousy, self-seeking. All
these Benedict sums up in the one expression *propriis voluntati-
bus*.[31] He expects his monks to put aside immediately their own
concerns and abandon their own wills at the call of obedience
(RB 5.7; 7.31). No one in the monastery is to follow his own heart's
desire (RB 3.8), for monks are not permitted to have even their
own bodies or wills at their disposal (RB 33.4). On the other hand,
during Lent Benedict invites them to offer to God of their own
will—*propria voluntate*—something above their assigned measure
(RB 49.6).

Following one's own will may seem to promise happiness;
Ælred ironically comments: "To those attached to their own wills
no food tastes better to the mind, none is relished more, none so
delights and cheers the spirit."[32] In reality, however, *voluntas
propria* is diametrically opposed to our true good. Saint Peter
Damian exclaims: "What tyrant is more cruel, what power more
violent to a person than his own will? . . . The more obediently

30. RM 90.41-43; CS 6:263.

31. By the plural form, Benedict suggests not so much the will itself as its
particular promptings and suggestions. See Timothy Fry, ed., *Rule of Saint Benedict 1980* (Collegeville, MN: Liturgical, Press, 1980), 157.

32. Quad 1; Ser Ined 56.

he obeys it, the more cruelly he is bound by its chains."[33] Gyrovagues are enslaved to their own wills (RB 1.11). "Within us," says Saint Bernard, "we have a castle that is opposed to us: that is our own will."[34] Elsewhere, he explains: "It is proper to God's eternally just law that he who does not want to accept its sweet rule will be the slave of his own will as a penance . . . and will have to bear unwillingly the unbearable burden of his own will."[35] Self-will "corrupts the heart and blinds the eyes of reason."[36] Seeking one's own will is tantamount to seeking one's own glory.[37] Ultimately, self-will leads to idolatry; it is "at enmity with God and wages a most relentless war against God . . . . As far as depends on it, it annihilates the Lord of Glory."[38]

* * *

From the foregoing consideration of *voluntas propria*, we are in a better position to appreciate its opposite. It seems to have been Saint Bernard who first coined the term *voluntas communis*[39]—common, that is, between God and ourselves. The accord of our will with God's is at the heart of the prayer Jesus gave his disciples: "May your will be done on earth as it is in heaven" (Matt 6:10) and at the heart of his own prayer, most explicitly at the time of his passion (Matt 26:42). Indeed, it was at the very heart of his mission and person: "I came not to do my own will, but the will of the One who sent me" (John 6:38).[40]

33. S for Saint Benedict.
34. Sent 3.12; CF 55:.198.
35. Dil 13.36; CF 13:128. Compare SC 82.5; CF 40:175.
36. Bernard, Res 2.8; Luddy 2:193.
37. Bernard, SC 4.3, CF 4:22; SC 24.8, CF 7:49; SC 19.7, CF 4:145.
38. Res 3.3; Luddy 2:202-3.
39. Res 2.8; Luddy 2:193.
40. Hans Urs von Balthasar brings out the profound implications of this idea in *Theo-Drama, Volume 2* (San Francisco: Ignatius, 1992), especially 183 ff. Jesus "is not in charge of himself; he has handed himself over to Another."

Even more simply, the opposite of *voluntas propria* is love,[41] the love that does not seek its own (1 Cor 13:5) but rather the good of others; the love to which Saint Paul exhorts the Corinthians (1 Cor 10:24) and the Philippians (Phil 2:4) and which he also practiced (1 Cor 13:33). It is this love that made the early Christian community one heart and one soul (Acts 4:32), the love that manifested itself in the sharing of possessions: "Neither did anyone say that any of the things he possessed was his own; but all things were common to all" (Acts 4:35).

These texts are constantly quoted and expanded on by subsequent writers. The apostolic fathers emphasize the aspect of community by using words with the prefix *syn*:

> "Attend the common meetings (*synerkomenoi*), and join in discussing (*synzeteite*) what contributes to the common good (*koiné sympherontos*)."[42]

> "Toil together, wrestle together, run together, suffer together, rise together" (all *syn-* words).[43]

Saint Gregory the Great commends those who leave their own interests, *propria*, to occupy themselves with the common good, *communio*.[44] He values the common good[45] and the common life[46] precisely because they are associated with love (*caritas*).

Writers on monastic life frequently refer to the text from Acts quoted above. For Cassian and for the whole tradition after him, as we shall see, it is in the primitive church of Jerusalem that the cenobitic life came into being:[47] "Monks alone maintain a lasting union in intimacy and possess all things in common, as they hold

41. Bernard equates *voluntas communis* with love: see Res 2.8; Luddy 2:193.
42. *Letter of Barnabas* 5.10; ACW 6:42.
43. Ignatius of Antioch, *Letter to Polycarp 6.1*; ACW 1:98.
44. Ir 4.99.1886; CCSL 144:344.
45. Ir 6.29.647, CCSL 144:565-6; Mo 5.27.27; CCSL 143:251-2.
46. Ir 6.29.643; CCSL 144:564.
47. Conl 18.5.1; Ramsey 637.

that everything that belongs to their brethren is their own, and that everything that is their own is their brethren's."[48]

Saint Augustine sums up his ideal of Christian community life in the lovely phrase "one mind and one heart in God."[49] In a letter to the young Lætus he develops his thought: monks renounce what is their own (*propria*) to facilitate achieving "our common treasure, which will last forever (*mansura communia*)." Those who renounce private affection gain "that union and sense of sharing of which it was said, 'They had but one soul and heart toward God.' Thus, your soul is not your own but is shared by all the brethren whose souls are also yours, or rather, whose souls form with yours not souls but one soul, the single soul of Christ."[50] Similarly, in his *Rule*, Augustine directs: "Make sure that no one is working for his own benefit, but that everything you do is for the common good, with more zeal and promptness than if each one of you were working for himself. For love, of which it is written that it is not self-seeking (1 Cor 13:5) must be understood as putting the common good before private interests, and not the other way round."[51]

Although Saint Benedict does not use the phrase *voluntas communis*, the ideal of a common will underlies his *Regula monasteriorum*. It would hardly be an exaggeration to say that all its prescriptions are designed both to foster and to express the common will. It is specifically written for cenobites (RB 1.2, 13), by definition those who live a common life. Worship (RB 8-19), sleep (RB 22), meals (RB 24) are all in common; all the goods of the monastery are to be the common possession of all (RB 33.6, quoting Acts 4:32). The whole community is involved in decision making (RB 3); to be excluded from the community to a greater or lesser degree is considered a severe punishment (RB 23–27).

48. Conl 24.26.3; Ramsey 848.
49. C Faust Manich 5. See Adolar Zumkeller, *Augustine's Ideal of the Religious Life* (New York: Fordham UP, 1986) [hereafter *Ideal*] 323.
50. Ep 243.3-4; FC 32:220-1.
51. Reg 5.2; *Ideal* 293.

Obedience is an effective way to conform to the Lord's saying: "I came not to do my own will, but the will of the One who sent me" (John 6:38). Doing only what is endorsed by the common rule of the monastery is the eighth step of humility. The ideals of mutual service (RB 35) and mutual obedience (RB 71), ideals that are present throughout the *Rule*, reach their culmination in chapter 72: "No one is to pursue what he judges better for himself, but instead, what he judges better for someone else" (RB 72.7, echoing 1 Cor 10:24, 33; Phil 2:4; Rom 12:10).

* * *

Desiring to live Saint Benedict's *Rule* in its fullness and steeped in its spirit, the early Cistercians had a strong sense of community. Saint Robert and the other founders, united "by common counsel [*communi consilio*] and common consent [*communi assensu*] strove to bring to perfection what they had conceived with one spirit," as the *Exordium Cistercii* tells us. Later, the "one rule and similar usages" imposed by the *Carta Caritatis* were meant to further the one love binding together all the daughters of the New Monastery, Cîteaux.

The unity and unanimity achieved by renouncing *voluntas propria* were frequently enjoined and extolled: "What is our hope, or joy, or crown of glory?" (1 Thess 2:19) asks Saint Bernard of his monks. "What indeed but your unity and unanimity."[52] Speaking to them on Christmas Eve, he tells them: "The third night watch is zeal for the preservation of concord and unity. You keep this when, in the community, you give the will of each of your brothers preference over your own."[53]

Idung of Prüfening also extols unity:

> Unity, whose mother is charity, makes of many hearts one heart and of many souls one soul. The first monks in the church were the early church herself, that is, those of whom

52. Mich 2.1; Luddy 3:325.
53. Vig Nat 3.6; Luddy 1:336.

it is written: "They were all of one heart and one soul." Their unanimity made them monks, and all monks their imitators. Hence it is that an expounder of the psalms, in commenting on that verse in which occur the words "He who makes them live in unanimity in the house" substitutes *monks* for *unanimity* and said, "He who makes monks live in the house."[54]

Saint Ælred's formula for communion of wills is *singula sunt omnium, omnia singulorum*: "Each of you, brothers, before entering the monastery, had a soul that was your own. And now, since you have been converted, the Holy Spirit has made, of all your hearts, one heart and one soul. This soul, our community, has all the virtues, and above all that unity and concord thanks to which all that belongs to each one in particular belongs to all, and what belongs to all belongs to each one."[55] This unity reaches its perfection in heaven.[56]

William of Saint-Thierry is more inclined to the eremitical than to community life, but he does commend the common observance of the monastery (*communis institutionis*), pointing out that by following it, the monk is freed from trouble and anxiety.[57] Thus, little by little, the monk learns "to take charge of himself, to plan his life, to set his behavior in order."[58]

"What singularity cannot embrace," says Gilbert of Hoyland, "community and charity do embrace. Let us seek then, in union of hearts, and we shall seek in unity of action."[59] Not only shall we seek, adds Isaac of Stella, "we shall all enjoy one and the same Good, that is, God, in common—this good, which is distributed to them, as appropriate to each one, by the One himself."[60]

54. *Cistercians and Cluniacs*, trans. Jeremiah F. O'Sullivan and others, CF 33:84. Idung is here quoting Augustine; see En in Ps 132.1-3; *Psalms* III/20:175-7.

55. OS 2, PL 195:347-8; see also Ben 3, PL 195:249; Spec car 2.17.43, CF 17:194.

56. Anima 3.47; CF 22:255.

57. Ep frat 1.19.75-76; CF 12:37.

58. Ep frat 1.28.107; CF 12:47.

59. Quer; CF 34:16.

60. S 50.20; SCh 339:194.

When we give up our own will, Bernard teaches, "we lose nothing; on the contrary, we gain a great deal, because our wills are not destroyed, but only changed for the better, so that what was *propria* becomes *communis*."[61] The perfection of union between God and the soul consists of "communion of wills and agreement in charity, *communio voluntatum et consensus in caritate*."[62] In fact, "*voluntas communis* is nothing but love."[63] Hence, whenever Bernard and the other Cistercians speak about love—and they do so constantly—*voluntas communis* is implied. If, as William says, "Love is nothing else than the will ardently fixed on the good,"[64] then when the will is freed from its *propria*, it "is now something more than a will"; it "reaches the stage at which it becomes love."[65]

None of the Cistercians, and perhaps no other medieval author, has written more eloquently or profoundly on *communis* than Baldwin of Forde, in his fifteenth tractate. Like his predecessors, he sees the common life of monks derived from the life of the early churches as described in the Acts, but he sees it more sublimely as "instituted by celestial models, brought down from heaven and adopted by us from the heavenly way of life of the holy angels,"[66] where "all want the same things and all are averse to the same things; what pleases one is displeasing to none, and what one wants, they all want. There is one purpose and one will for all; all feel the same thing, and all sense the same thing . . . .What is proper to each is common to all."[67] Yet there is a still more sublime exemplar of common life, that of God himself, the life of the blessed Trinity, where "just as [the three persons] have one common essence and one common nature, so they have one common life."[68]

61. Res 2.8; Luddy 2:183.
62. SC 71:10; CF 40:56.
63. Res 2.8; Luddy 2:193.
64. Nat am 4; CF 30:56.
65. Ep frat 2.14-15; CF 12:92-94.
66. S 15.3; T 15, CF 41:157.
67. S 15.23-4; T 15; CF 41:164-5.
68. S 15.5, T 15; CF 41:158.

Baldwin distinguishes three kinds of sharing, *communio*: those of nature, grace, and glory.[69] Love of neighbor is based on the nature we have in common; if we do not love our neighbor, we do not truly love ourselves either.[70] Something more, however, is needed for the common life of a monastic community: a communion of grace: "From the fellowship (*communicatione*) of the Holy Spirit comes that communion that is essential to those who live communally.[71] Baldwin goes on to describe the ideal of cenobitic life in a passage full of allusions to the *Rule* of Saint Benedict:

> Since they have but one heart and one soul (Ac 4:32) and all things in common, there is concord and unanimity (*concordia et unanimitas*) throughout, and they always put the general profit and the common good before their own individual convenience. They so far renounce themselves and what is theirs that none of them, if indeed he is [truly] one of them, whether in [making] decisions or in [giving] advice, presumes to make a stubborn defense of his own opinion, nor to strive hard after his own will and the desires of his own heart, nor to have the least thing that could be called his own. Instead, as servants of God, they humble themselves for the sake of God under the hand of one of their fellow-servants, and in him all power is vested. His judgment alone determines the decisions, regulates the will, and governs the needs of all. He alone can want something or refuse it, for the others have renounced their own power and freedom [of will]. Thus, they are not permitted to want

69. S 15.26, T 15; CF 41:165.

70. S 15.30, T 15; CF 41:167.

71. S 15.51, T 15; CF 41:174. In another place, Baldwin relates this *communicatio* to the Eucharist:
> "The chalice of benediction that we bless, is it not a sharing [*communicatio*] in the blood of Christ (1 Cor 10:16)?" It is a sharing, because it is given and received in common; a communion (*communio*), because it is possessed in common. It can also be called communion for another reason: the blood effects in us that charity by which all things become common, and what belongs to each becomes common to all. (Sac alt 2.4; SCh 94:358)

what they want, nor to be able [to do] what they are able [to do], nor to feel what they feel, nor to be what they are, nor to live by their own spirit, but by the Spirit of God. It is he who leads them to be sons of God (Rm 8:14), and it is he who is their love, their bond, and their communion. The greater their love, the stronger is their bond and the more perfect is their communion: and conversely, the greater their communion, the stronger is their bond and the more perfect is their love.[72]

Baldwin poses a problem. If, according to Acts 4:32, "they had everything in common," how can this assertion be reconciled with the following verse: "Distribution was made to each one according to his need"? The solution is that "by its judgment, charity knows how to convert individual ownership by making individual ownership serve a common end (*ut proprietas ad communionem conducat*)."[73]

This, therefore, is the law of the common life: unity of spirit in the charity of God, the bond of peace in the mutual unfailing charity of all the brethren, the sharing of all the good that should be shared, and the total rejection of any idea of personal ownership in the way of life of holy religion.[74]

This communion and sharing extend to all the members of the Church, on earth and in heaven; this communion of saints, and it is on their merits that Baldwin relies to make good his own sufficiency:

We need not be distressed in our heart; we need not be confined by the boundaries and limits of our insignificant righteousness. Charity extends our hope to the communion of the saints, and we can, therefore, share with them their

72. S 15.44, T 15; CF 41:171.
73. S 15.67-69, T 15; CF 41:181-2.
74. S 15.51, T 15; CF 41:177. This passage is quoted in the new *Constitutions* of the monks and nuns of the Cistercian Order of the Strict Observance (Rome, 1990); see Cst 13.1.

merits [in this present time] and their rewards in the time
to come, sharing in the glory that shall be revealed to us
. . . . It is then that God shall wipe away all the tears from
the eyes of his saints (Rv 21:4). It is then that all the saints will
be as one heart and one soul, and they will have all things in
common when God will be all in all (1 Cor 15:28).[75]

Étienne Gilson gives a lucid explanation of the teaching of
the Cistercians, indeed of the whole tradition, on *voluntas propria*
and *voluntas communis*:

What is the object of the Cistercian ascesis? Progressively
to eliminate the *proprium* in order to install charity in its
place. What is this *proprium*? Unlikeness—in virtue of which
[the human being] will be different from God. But what, on
the other hand, is [the human being]? A divine likeness. It
is, therefore, perfectly clear that in such a doctrine there is
a coincidence between the loss of "proper will" and the
restoration of our true nature. To eliminate from self all that
stands in the way of being really oneself, that is not to lose,
but to find oneself once more.[76]

When this is accomplished:

instead of willing a thing out of fear of another, or of willing
a thing out of covetousness for something else, [the will] is
now enabled, having chosen the sole object that can be
willed for itself, to tend toward it with a direct and simple
movement, in short with a "spontaneous" movement. . . .
Love, making the will spontaneous, also makes it voluntary
(in French, *volonté*, *volontiers*), restores it to itself, makes it
become once more a will.[77]

---

75. S 15.89-90, T 15; CF 41:191.

76. ET: Étienne Gilson, *The Mystical Theology of Saint Bernard*, trans. A. H. C.
Downes, CS 120:128.

77. Gilson 90.

Chapter 2

THE MOTHER OF VIRTUES

Discretio

Discernment is a word and a concept much used today, and with good reason. It has a very practical value. If our fundamental moral obligation is to avoid evil and choose good, we must first know what is good and what is evil. This is precisely the function of discernment; beyond general norms, it shows us how to decide on the right course of action in specific circumstances. The Latin verb *cernere* can mean either to separate or to see, the two meanings come together in *discernere*: to see deeply in order to separate, distinguish or discern.

Discernere, which has a long history in Christian tradition, has kept its original meaning. The meaning of discretion, on the other hand, has been somewhat weakened over the centuries—today it usually carries connotations of excessive reserve and caution. Yet *discretio* is the past participle of *discernere*; discretion is the result of a correct discernment.

Discretio as used in the Vulgate generally refers to judgment. In two significant texts it comes closer to a more specific power of discernment. Solomon asks God to: "Give your servant an understanding heart, to judge your people, and discern between good and evil." The letter to the Hebrews speaks of the mature, or perfect as "those who have their senses trained by practice to distinguish good from evil" (Heb 5:14). The first text puts the emphasis on discretion as God's gift; the second adds the notion of human activity.

The concept of discernment occurs in a number of places in the New Testament without the word itself being used; for example, 1 Thessalonians 5:21-22: "Test everything, hold fast what is good, abstain from every form of evil"; Romans 12:2: "Be reformed in the newness of your mind, that you may prove what is the will of God, what is good and acceptable and perfect"; 1 John 4:1: "Test the spirits to see whether they are from God." The Council of Jerusalem (Acts 15) is a practical example of community discernment. Paul, playing with the words *hyperphronein*, *phronein*, and *sophronein*, warns the Romans "Not to be more wise than it behooves to be wise, but to be wise unto sobriety," (Rom 12:3) and urges the Philippians to let their moderation—forebearance, *epieikes*—be known to all (Phil 4:5).[1]

* * *

For Origen, discretion is needed in order to come to self-knowledge[2] and to discover the source of our thoughts.[3] Beginners in the spiritual life are distinguished from the "perfect" by the criterion of Hebrews 5:14; the latter are able to discern between good and evil. Only they are qualified to read the Song of Songs.[4] They have been trained by learning and diligence and much experience[5] and are now capable of receiving solid food (Heb 5:13); to them, Christ reveals himself more fully.[6]

In general, however, patristic writers used *discretio* in its primary sense of division, separation, distinction; for example, the separation of light from darkness on the first day of creation;[7]

---

1. Paul's list of charismatic gifts in 1 Corinthians 12 includes that of discernment of spirits: *diakrisis pneumaton; discretio spirituum*. This phrase became a technical term; while related to discretion, it is different enough to require a study of its own.

2. Comm in cant 2.5.16; ACW 26:132.

3. Peri arch 3.2-4; ANF 4:331-6.

4. Comm in cant Pro 1.4; ACW 26:22.

5. Comm in cant 1.4.18; ACW 26:80.

6. Comm in cant 1.4.13; ACW 26:78.

7. Augustine, De Gen ad lit 1.10.19; ACW 41:30.

the separation of good and evil at the judgment of God;[8] distinction between divine and human things;[9] the distinction of persons in the Trinity.[10]

* * *

It is in the monastic movement of the fourth and fifth centuries that *discretio* comes into its own. The question that one monk continually asked another, particularly an elder, was: "What must I do to be saved?" The sayings that have come down to us as their responses to this question constitute a veritable treatise on discretion, even when the word is not used. But in fact there is a lengthy chapter in the *Verba Seniorum* specifically devoted to that subject. A homely example illustrates the necessity of discretion: "Abba Ammonas said, 'A man can spend his whole time carrying an ax without succeeding in cutting down the tree, while another, with experience of tree-felling brings the tree down with a few blows.' He said that the ax is discretion."[11] Without discretion, austerities, no matter how severe, are of no avail: "Some have afflicted their bodies with asceticism, but they lack discretion, and so they are far from God."[12]

Being concerned with making as radical a response as possible to the demands of Christianity, in lieu of the martyrdom that was no longer a likelihood, the early monks were from the start inclined to an idealism which could easily lead to extreme measures, even to trying to outdo one another in ascetic practices. In the beginning, every kind of experiment and excess was tried. Experience taught the need of moderation—discretion—and also of relying on the counsels of those who had already lived the

8. Augustine, In Joan 19.18.1; FC 79:159.

9. Hilary, De trin 12.20; FC 25:514-5.

10. Hilary, De trin 2.31; FC 25:60.

11. *Western Asceticism*, trans. Owen Chadwick (Philadelphia: Westminster, 1958), 117. Henceforth, Chadwick.

12. Chadwick, 105.

monastic life. For example, rather than fasting for days on end, monks are advised to eat every day, but a little less than they would like.[13] Their manner of life should be in accord with their capabilities: a monk who asks: "Is it good not to have any comfort in one's cell? I saw a brother who had a few cabbages, and he was rooting them out" is told: "It is good. But each one should do what is right for his own discipline. If he has not the strength to endure that, he will plant them again."[14] Thus, different advice on the same subject is given, depending on the questioner. One monk asks about temptations, and is told to let them in, and then fight them. Another monk, asking the same question, is told to cut them off straightaway.[15]

In a broader context, discretion could consist in doing the loving thing, even if it might go counter to established protocol:

> Some old men were entertaining themselves at Scetis by having a meal together; amongst them was Abba John. A venerable priest got up to offer drink, but nobody accepted any from him, except John the Dwarf. They were surprised and said to him: "How is it that you, the youngest, dared to let yourself be served by the priest?" Then he said to them: "When I get up to offer drink, I am glad when everyone accepts it, since I am receiving my reward; that is the reason, then, that I accepted it, so that he also might gain his reward and not be grieved by seeing that no one would accept anything from him." When they heard this, they were all filled with wonder and edification at his discretion.[16]

* * *

It was John Cassian who, in his *Institutes* and *Conferences*, gathered together, synthesized and transmitted to the monks of

---

13. Chadwick, 115.
14. Chadwick, 106.
15. Chadwick, 111.
16. CS 59:74.

Europe the teaching of the Desert Fathers. His teaching on discretion reflects theirs.

Cassian begins his first Conference by establishing the goal of the monastic life: ultimately, the kingdom of heaven; proximately, purity of heart or holiness (which he will later equate with contemplation).[17] This leads quite naturally into the subject of discretion, which encompasses all the practical means to attain the desired goal.

While the Conferences taken as a whole can be viewed as an extended exercise in discretion, the latter part of the first Conference, and all of the second, are entirely devoted to it. Cassian assures us that discretion is not a human quality, but "among the noblest gifts of the Spirit."[18] It "sees and casts light," not only on all a person's thoughts, but also on his actions, "discerning everything that must be done" or avoided.[19] It "teaches the monk always to proceed along the royal road, avoiding the extremes of either presumption or lukewarmness.[20] From the examples given later, it seems that presumption was the more frequent danger for the early monks, but in the end, one extreme is as bad as the other; in fact, excessive abstinence is worse than eating too much[21] as being a more subtle temptation.

Discretion, however, must go deeper than behavior. Since purity of heart is our goal, and since the heart is the source of our thoughts, we need to know how to discern and judge them:

> With a wise discretion we should examine all the thoughts that emerge in our heart, first tracing their origins and causes and their authors, so that, in accordance with the status of whoever is suggesting them, we may be able to consider how we should approach them.[22]

17. Conl 1.1-8; Ramsey 41-48.
18. Conl 2.1.3; Ramsey 83.
19. Conl 2.2.5; Ramsey 85.
20. Conl 2.2.4; Ramsey 85.
21. Conl 2.17.1; Ramsey 100.
22. Conl 1.20.1; Ramsey 59.

They may come from God, the devil, or ourselves, and Cassian goes on to explain the art of discerning their origins, which is comparable to that of judging the value of coins.

The question then becomes: how is this great quality to be obtained? Only by true humility, Cassian replies. And

> the first proof of this humility will be if not only everything that is to be done, but also everything that is thought of is offered to the inspection of the elders, so that not trusting in one's own judgment, one may submit in every respect to their understanding and may know how to judge what is good and bad according to what they have handed down.[23]

Indeed, the very act of revealing the thoughts will deliver one from their power.

If Cassian lays so much importance on relying on another's judgment, it is surely because he knows how easy it is to deceive oneself about the source and goodness of what comes into one's mind. However, discretion must also be exercised in choosing an elder to whom one may submit his thoughts. One's own personal discernment comes into play here. Some monks have a special grace for discretion.[24] The criterion to be used is this: "Only those elders who have shaped their own lives in a praiseworthy and upright manner are to be followed," for an elder who is lacking in the compassion that comes from experiencing his own weakness may wound a younger monk who confides in him, instead of encouraging and healing him.[25]

Nothing militates against discretion more than anger, for "If we are angry for any reason at all, good or bad, we will at once lose the light of discretion"[26] and "What could be more tragic than that a person should lose the ability to judge what is good, and the rule and discipline of a careful discretion."[27]

23. Conl 2.10.1; Ramsey 90.
24. Inst 5.4; NPF 11:234.
25. Conl 2.13; Ramsey 94-98.
26. Inst 8.21; NPF 11:263.
27. Conl 19.14.6; Ramsey 680.

Since Cassian perceives discretion as the passing of wisdom from generation to generation, it is appropriate that he gives the teaching of Anthony of the Desert and other earlier monks when describing its excellence. It is

> that which would lead the fearless monk on a steady ascent to God, and which would always preserve [the other] virtues undamaged; that with which the heights of perfection could be scaled with little weariness; that without which many of those who labor even with a good will would be unable to arrive at the summit.[28]

In brief: "Discretion is the begetter, guardian and moderator of all virtues."[29]

* * *

Since the sayings of the Desert Fathers and the writings of Cassian were among the major sources of the *Rule* of Saint Benedict, it is not surprising to find that, like them, it is characterized by a spirit of discretion. In the Prologue Benedict expresses the hope that his *Rule* will contain nothing harsh or burdensome (RB Prol. 46). and he is always at pains to allow for human weaknesses; those of the very young and the elderly (RB 37.2-3) of the sick, (RB 36) of those who have special needs, (RB 55.21) and even of those who are unable to spend Sundays in study or reading (RB 48.23).

The influence of Cassian's teaching on discretion is evident in many places in the *Rule*; for example, the revelation of thoughts to the abbot (RB 7.44, 46.5-6), and the stress placed on following the example of the seniors, the teaching of the holy fathers (RB 7.55, 73.2).

Discretion is a quality particularly needed by the abbot, who must be able to "serve a variety of temperaments, coaxing, reproving and encouraging them as appropriate. He must accommodate

28. Conl 2.4.3; Ramsey 87.
29. Conl 2.4.3; Ramsey 87.

and adapt himself to each one's character and intelligence" (RB 31–32); some will respond to convincing argument, some to appeal, others only to reproof and rebuke (RB 2.25). In correcting the brethren he must not go to extremes lest by rubbing too hard to remove the rust, he may break the vessel (RB 64.12). Moreover, he

> must show forethought and consideration in his orders, and whether the task he assigns concerns God or the world, he should be discerning and moderate, bearing in mind the discretion of holy Jacob, who said: "If I drive my flocks too hard, they will all die in a single day" (Gn 33.13). Therefore, drawing on this and other examples of discretion, the mother of virtues, he must so arrange everything that the strong have something to yearn for and the weak nothing to run from. (64.17-19)

This last sentence makes it clear that Benedict does not equate discretion with the least common denominator. Those who are able are encouraged to make their whole monastic life a continual Lent, though Benedict realizes that few have the strength for this (RB 49.1). In any case, he recognizes that outward austerities have only relative importance in the journey to God. He puts no limit on the virtues he recommends to his monks. They are not merely to walk but to run in the ways of the Lord (RB Prol. 49) while they have the light of life (RB Prol. 13; John 12:35); to desire everlasting life with all the passion (*concupiscentia*, a strong word) of the spirit (RB 4.46); to hasten to the heavenly homeland (RB 73.8); to aspire to loftier summits of teaching and virtue than he himself provides (RB 73.9). One might conclude that the essence of Benedictine discretion is choosing the most efficacious and direct way to one's goal.

* * *

Pope Saint Gregory the Great lived under the *Rule* of Saint Benedict, and when he came to speak of it in the *Dialogues*, singled out discretion as its most notable characteristic.[30] But Gregory had

30. Di 2:36; FC 39:107.

not only admired the *Rule's* discretion; he had made it his own, so it is not surprising that he gives it an important place in his own writings. Jean Leclercq has given him the title "doctor of desire." An equally apt title would seem to be "doctor of discretion."

Gregory, like Benedict, regards discretion as a particularly important quality for anyone in a position of authority, above all for a pastor. His *Pastoral Care*, which had such a great influence in the Middle Ages, is a practical handbook on the art of discernment, choosing the appropriate response to specific persons and situations. The wise must be treated differently than the dull, the impudent than the timid, the insolent than the fainthearted, the impatient than the patient, and so on.

Discretion for Gregory, as for Benedict, never becomes merely a matter of moderation, although it may include that. It is above all a question of choosing the right direction. True discretion demands of each one the best he is capable of. Discretion complements *theoria*, contemplative knowledge. It is, in fact, the voice of conscience.

Gregory often uses discretion with a word which underlines its meaning as a thoughtful judgment, resulting in a correct evaluation; such words as *rationis, principatuum*,[31] *mentis discretion*.[32] Discretion is a light,[33] a scale.[34] Even the gift of piety "is useless if it lacks *scientiae discretionis*, the gift of knowledge, for without knowledge, piety knows not how to act mercifully."[35] By an attentive discretion, one must become little enough to be able to enter the narow gate that leads to life.[36] Commenting on Job 1:16, "I alone have escaped," Gregory states that whatever the soul may suffer at the hands of its enemies, if discretion alone remains, all can be regained. In fact, "The mind's discernment grows stronger in the face of temptations by learning how to distinguish

31. Mo 1.30.42; SCh 32;226.
32. Mo 2.29.79; SCh 32:376.
33. Mo 28.11.30; PL 76:465.
34. Mo 3.13.24; PL 75:611.
35. Mo 1.32.45; SCh 32:230.
36. Mo 28.11.26; PL 76:463.

more precisely between virtues and vices."[37] Hence he speaks of the citadel of discretion, which comes with the wisdom of maturity.[38]

With his penchant for vivid metaphors, Gregory speaks of discretion as a hand that brushes away evil thoughts,[39] as the finger placed on one's mouth (Job 21:5) to prevent rash speech,[40] as the heel under which pride may be trampled.[41] Discretion is the cloven hoof of a calf (Ezek 1:7)—in this case, knowing when to understand Scripture literally, and when to look for an allegorical meaning.[42] Discretion is a mean between excessive rigor and undue lenience, combining the gentleness of the ox and the fierceness of the lion: an allusion to 1 Kings 7:29, which describes the lions and the oxen carved upon the stands in the temple.[43]

Nowhere is Gregory's conception of discretion more graphically presented than when he draws upon Leviticus 21:17-21, which excludes anyone who has a blemish . . . or has a little, or a great, or a crooked nose from offering sacrifices to the Lord: "A man with a little nose is one who is incapable of discernment, for by the nose we discern sweet odors from stench. Rightly, then, the nose symbolizes discretion, whereby we choose virtue and reject sin." It is, however, possible to carry discretion too far: "Some fall into error by their excessive subtlety. Hence the addition, 'a great and crooked nose.' Evidently, [this means] immoderate subtlety in making distinctions; when this develops inordinately, it distorts the correctness of its own functioning."[44] So we return to discretion as a mean between two extremes.

37. Mo 2.46.73-2.50.80; SCh 32:362-378.
38. Mo 11.46.62; SCh 212:128.
39. Mo 16.42.53; SCh 221:216.
40. Mo 15.37.43; SCh 221:76.
41. Mo 27.46.77; PL 76:444.
42. Hiez 1.3.4; Gray 32.
43. Hiez 2.9.18; Gray 270.
44. Reg Past 1.11; ACW 11:41.

* * *

The monastic tradition continues to speak of *discretio* as moderation; for example this passage from a work attributed to Saint Anselm:

> Abstinence must be discreet, proportioned to one's temperament and physical strength; otherwise, far from being a help, it will be a great hindrance. Someone riding a horse has two reins—if he pulls one more than the other, the horse won't go straight ahead. The two reins are self-indulgence and excessive austerity.[45]

But when writing philosophically, Anselm takes a much broader view of discretion, seeing it as the raison d'être of our faculty of reason:

> We should not doubt that the rational nature was created just by God, so that it might be blessed in the enjoyment of him. For it is rational for the very purpose of distinguishing the just from the not-just, the good from the not-good, the greater good from the lesser. . . . It received the power of discernment so that it might hate and shun evil, and love and choose the good—and love and choose the greatest good most of all. For otherwise God would have given it the power of discernment in vain, since it would distinguish in vain if it did not love and avoid in the light of its *discrimination*.[46]

* * *

The Cistercians, since they presuppose the whole previous monastic tradition, do not find it necessary to mention discretion explicitly very often. Nevertheless, the concept underlies their approach to the spiritual life. Saint Bernard calls it "the mother of virtues and the crown of perfection. By it we are taught to avoid excess in everything. . . . [It] keeps us between the ex-

---

45. *De similitudinibus*, 193; PL 159:704 (translation mine).
46. Cur 2.1; *A Scholastic Miscellany: Anselm to Ockham*, ed. Eugene R. Fairweather (Philadelphia: Westminster, 1956), 196–97.

tremes of too much and too little."[47] Those who lack discretion, observes Saint Ælred,

> neglect important matters but are aroused at all minute points. They confuse everything without regarding the fitting place, the due season. . . . Anyone who lacks discretion is like a ship bereft of its pilot, borne along by every shifting and irrational movement.[48]

Although discretion keeps one on the middle course, there is always the danger that balance and moderation may degenerate into mediocrity, tepidity, self-indulgence. Bernard takes obvious delight in satirizing such a false concept of discretion:

> Things have come to such a pass that right order and religion are thought to be promoted, the more concern and pleasure and enthusiasm there is regarding such things [as food, clothing, buildings]. Abstemiousness is accounted miserliness, sobriety strictness, silence gloom. On the other hand, laxity is labeled discretion, extravagance generosity, talkativeness sociability, and laughter joy. Fine clothes and costly caparisons are regarded as mere respectability, and being fussy about bedding is hygiene. When we lavish these things on one another, we call it love. Such love undermines true love. Such discretion disgraces real discretion. This sort of kindness is full of cruelty, for it so looks after the body that the soul is strangled. How can love pamper the flesh and neglect the spirit? What sort of discretion is it to give everything to the body and nothing to the soul? Is it kindness to entertain the maid and murder the mistress? . . . [This is] not mercy but cruelty; it is not love but malevolence not discretion but disorder [*non est caritas, sed iniquitas, non est discretio, sed confusio*].[49]

This is merely "worldly wisdom masquerading in the dress and name of discretion."[50] True discretion, as Ælred sees it, "is to

---

47. Circ 3.11; Luddy 1:446; cf. John of Forde, S 77.2; CF 45:186.
48. Spir am 3.72-3; CF 5:108-9.
49. Apol 16-17; CF 1:53-4.
50. SC 30:12; CF 7:123.

put the soul before the body, and where both are threatened and the health of the one can only be obtained at the price of suffering for the other, to neglect the body for the sake of the soul."[51]

Since true discretion is "a rare bird on earth," Bernard advises his monks to "let the virtue of obedience supply for it."[52] William of Saint-Thierry puts it forcefully: "The whole discernment of a novice ought to be to make himself a fool in all things for Christ (1 Cor 4:10) and to depend on the judgment of another."[53] He explains this more fully to the Carthusians of Mont Dieu:

> Perfect obedience, especially in a beginner, does not include discretion. . . . For the tree which gives knowledge of good and evil in paradise (Gn 2.9) is in religious life the power to decide, and it is entrusted to the spiritual father who judges all things while he himself is judged by no one. . . . It is impossible for one who, in the "animal" state, decides for himself, a "prudent" novice, a "wise" beginner, to stay in his cell for long or to persevere in the community. Let him become foolish if he is to be wise, and let this be the whole of his discretion, to be entirely without discretion in this.[54]

Bernard agrees that the spirit of discernment is particularly needed by those in authority, so that "aptly suiting themselves to the occasion, they may know how to exercise zeal at the proper time and also how at the proper time to show compassion."[55] Discretion is the moderator between zeal and mercy: "When the eye of discretion in blinded, it is usual for zeal and mercy each to seize a place for itself and occupy it. Discretion is blinded by two things: anger and extreme soft heartedness."[56]

If discernment enables us to distinguish our thoughts, good and evil, it is liable to error, warns Baldwin of Forde:

51. Inst 23; CF 2:70.
52. Circ 3:11; Luddy 1:446.
53. Nat am 7; CF 30:59-60.
54. Ep frat 53-4; CF 12:30-31.
55. Pasch 2:6; Luddy 2:192.
56. Csi 2:20; CF 37:74-5.

There exist certain imitations both of true virtues and of vices which delude the eyes of the heart and which so beguile the keen-eyed mind with their illusions that what is really not good may have every appearance of being good, and what is really not wicked may have every appearance of being wicked.[57]

It is only the Lord who knows all the thoughts and intentions of our heart (Heb 4:12). So Baldwin exclaims:

Who can test whether the spirits are from God (1 Jn 4.1) save he who is granted by God [the grace] of discernment of spirits, who can thereby examine with accuracy and true judgment spiritual thoughts, affection and intentions? Discernment is the mother of the virtues, and it is essential for every individual, whether it be for governing the lives of others or the direction and correction of one's own [life]. But the only word that can introduce this into our sense is that living and effective [Word] who is the discerner of the thoughts and intentions of the heart.[58]

If discretion is needed to avoid laxity, it is just as necessary for restraining the overly zealous. "Where zeal is enthusiastic, there discretion, that moderator *ordinatio* of love, is especially necessary."[59] In one of his Parables—allegories in which he describes the way to God in terms of the knighthood with which his young monks were familiar—Bernard gives a vivid description of Prudence restraining the ardor of the impetuous horse named Desire with the bridle of Discretion, and giving the reins into the control of Temperance.[60] Putting it another way, Baldwin sees that

zeal should be united with knowledge and knowledge with zeal. There will then be no devotion without discernment

57. S 18:81; T 6; CF 38:183.
58. S 18:81-83; T 6; CF 38:184.
59. Bernard, SC 49:5; CF 31:5.
60. Par 1:4; CF 55:21.

nor discernment without devotion. . . . Devotion without
discernment generally [involves] tempting God with the
temptation of impossible things, and because it does not
know which things are profitable, it either presumes [to do]
what is not expedient or neglects [to do] what is expedient.
But in the case of discernment without devotion, although
it makes no mistake in knowing what things are profitable,
it is mistaken in what it chooses.[61]

William, perhaps the most introspective of the Cistercians,
links discretion with self-knowledge:

Know yourself—be ready for discernment in your own regard. . . . Be wholly present to yourself, and employ yourself
wholly in knowing yourself and knowing whose image you
are, and likewise in discerning and understanding what you
are and what you can do in him whose image you are.[62]

This knowledge will grow as the soul makes progress:

[After] the bride has been instructed through the Master's
chastisement and correction and glorified by the gift of wisdom, she begins to know herself more perfectly and to
understand and discern what is taking place within her.[63]

But since for William, knowing oneself is the way to knowing
the One in whose image we are made, we find him longing to
"discern the love of God more deeply." He laments that his
understanding "is not allowed to remain in the light of [God's]
countenance" (Ps 88:16) long enough to do so.[64] Yet in the final
analysis—and this is an insight characteristic not only of William
but of all the Cistercians—what God's love truly is cannot be
discerned by the intelligence; this can be done "only by the *affectus*," that is, by the heart.[65]

61. S 3:61-2; T 11; CF 41:114.
62. Exp 66; CF 6:52-3.
63. Exp 74; CF 6:62.
64. Med 12:11; CF 3:172.
65. Med 12:18; CF 3:173.

Ordinatio, order, is an important concept for the Cistercians; a favorite text is Song 2:4: "he set love in order in me." And they see this ordering as precisely the role of discretion. John of Forde, for example, calls it "the balanced judgment that . . . keeps [the bride] as it were balanced between both extremes, that is ecstatic joy and grief, so that she falls into neither danger."[66]

Even charity requires the help of discretion, which

> restrains within fixed limits, the excesses and ardent impulses of [every single virtue, indeed of] charity itself. Certainly charity is sovereign. She is rightly called the queen of the virtues, and so she is. All the same, though, charity herself does not escape the control of discretion, and she humbly submits herself to it to be regulated and kept in check. In fact, this is the very reason why charity trusts that her kingdom will last for ever, this it is ordered by the very just laws laid down by the ripe wisdom of discretion.[67]

> Though discretion is needed to order charity, it is not a substitute for it: Without the fervor of charity, the virtue of discretion is lifeless, and intense fervor goes headlong without the curb of discretion. Praiseworthy the one who possesses both the fervor that enlivens discretion and the discretion that regulates fervor.[68]

Bernard sums up the thought of all the Cistercians on the necessity and value of discretion when he call it "not so much a virtue as a moderator and guide of the virtues, a director of the affections, a teacher of right living. Take it away and virtue becomes vice."[69]

---

66. S 46:6; CF 43:197.
67. S 77:9; CF 45:194-5.
68. Bernard, SC 23:8; CF 7:32.
69. SC 49:5; CF 31:25.

Chapter 3

PONDERING THE WORD

Meditare and *Ruminare*

To ponder, to ruminate, to reflect deeply and at length on a given subject—everything implied by the word meditation—is a fundamental human characteristic, found particularly in thoughtful people and rightly given prominence in worldwide religious traditions. Not surprisingly, then, the concept of meditation is deeply rooted in the Old Testament. Found chiefly in the psalms and the other Wisdom literature, this concept is expressed in terms derived from the root *haga*. Meditation is the occupation of those who are just (Ps 1:2; 36:30). In its primitive sense, a sense that persisted into the Middle Ages, *meditare* means 'to murmur in a low voice,' but also, and more profoundly, the heart is understood as the place of meditation (Ps 18:15; 48:4). The object of meditation is the Law, and it is meant to lead to ruling one's life by the Law. Conversely, there can also be an evil kind of meditation, directed to vain things (Ps 2:1), discord (Prov 17:19), or robberies (Prov 24:2).

The translation of the Hebrew term by *meletan* in Greek and *meditare* in Latin already implies an extension of meaning. The Greek term means 'to take care of,' to 'to watch over,' and especially 'to take to heart.' The Latin term has an even wider field of applications, from practicing a piece of music or a speech to handling weapons. "It often implies an affinity with the practical or even moral order."[1] When applied to reading a text, it means "to learn it 'by heart' in the fullest sense of this expression; it

---

1. "Meditation," DSp 10:906-14.

implies the use of one's memory, that fixes it, with the intelligence that understands its meaning, and with the will that desires to put it into practice."[2]

In the New Testament "to meditate" [*meditare*] is found only in the First Letter to Timothy 4:15, and then without special significance. Luke, however, presents Mary as a perfect model of meditation when he tells us that she kept all these words, pondering them in her heart (Luke 2:19, 50).

Christian meditation, in the tradition of the Old Testament, is oriented toward the Word of God, source of human nourishment and human life (Matt 4:4). With its object being the interiorization of the Word, meditation early on became linked to rumination, a homely but telling image of the process of assimilating the Word, derived from an allegorical interpretation of Leviticus 11:3 and Deuteronomy 14:6, where ruminants are classified among the clean animals. This association is already found in the *Epistle of Barnabas*[3] and is taken over by Clement of Alexandria[4] and other early Christian writers so that it becomes traditional. For example, Saint Augustine explains: "When you listen to [the Word of God], when you read it, you are eating it; when you meditate on it afterwards, you are ruminating, to prove yourself a clean animal, not an unclean one."[5]

John Cassian speaks of *meditatio cordis* and *incessabilis ruminatio* in the same breath.[6] It is a task both of mouth and of heart.[7] Meditation places the soul in a climate of spontaneous prayer: "Give yourself over assiduously or rather continuously to sacred reading, until continual meditation fills your heart and fashions

2. Jean Leclercq, *The Love of Learning and the Desire for God* (New York: Fordham UP, 1961), 20–22.

3. 10; FC 1:208.

4. *Pedagogue* 3:11:76; FC 23:257.

5. En in Ps 36, Ser 3.5; ACW 30:309.

6. Conl 14.13; 11.15; Ramsey 517-8. 422.

7. Inst 2.15; NPNF, 2nd series (Grand Rapids: Eerdmans, 1955) 11:211. Hereafter *Institutes*.

you so to speak after its own likeness."[8] The verse Cassian recommends above all others is "Come to my help, O God; Lord, hurry to my rescue" Ps 69:2). He eloquently explains the reasons for his choice:

> It carries within it all the feelings of which human nature is capable. It can be adapted to every condition and can be usefully deployed against every temptation. It carries within it a cry of help in the face of every danger. It expresses the humility of a pious confession. It conveys the watchfulness born of unending worry and fear. It conveys a sense of our frailty, the assurance of being heard, the confidence in help that is always and everywhere present.[9]

With equal eloquence Cassian describes the results of meditation:

> If its subjects are carefully received, if they are hidden and consigned within the quiet places of the mind, if they are marked in silence, they will later be like a wine of sweet aroma bringing gladness to the heart. Matured by long reflection and by patience, subjects will be poured out as a great fragrance from the vessel of your heart. . . . And so it will happen that not only the whole thrust and thought of your heart, but even all the wanderings and strayings of your thoughts will turn into a holy and unending meditation on the Law of God.[10]

Saint Benedict is more succinct, but he does expect his monks to spend the time after the night office in meditation, if they need a better knowledge of the psalms and lessons (RB 48.13), so it may be assumed that he is using *meditare* in the sense of *lectio* or study. Meditation or reading is to occupy the monks on Sundays (RB 48.23). But the most intensive time of meditation is to be that of the novitiate: "What the novice is meant to accomplish in the novitiate is defined in the *Rule* as meditation" (RB 58.5). This

---

8. Inst 2.14.10; *Institutes* 211.
9. Conl 10.10; Ramsey 379.
10. Conl 14.13; Ramsey 517.

practice involves the repetition of a text aloud, in order to learn it by heart: "Its goal was not purely intellectual but an existential appropriation of the Word in view of forming one's life"[11] and developing a contemplative outlook.

As meditation is nourished by reading and is meant to lead to prayer, the triad *lectio, meditatio, oratio* becomes a commonplace in the monastic tradition. At some point a fourth element was added: *contemplatio*. These four steps are found in Saint Bernard[12] and later described by Guigo II, the Carthusian, as four stages, steps, or rungs that lead the devout soul towards union with God.[13] For the medieval mind, however, these stages were considered as four aspects of the same reality, so that meditation often includes, at least by implication, the later stages.

The meaning and importance that the Cistercians attach to meditation can be gauged from the adjectives they use to describe it: it is devout[14] and holy;[15] it should be frequent;[16] and indeed continuous—"One meditation follows another, each helping the other with identical support and mutual aid"[17]—as well as pure[18] and earnest.[19] If at first it is laborious, "it is succeeded by the bliss of contemplation."[20] In meditation, "God's commandments become sweet, for we consider how beneficial they are, how upright how faithful, and how they are established for ever and ever, made in truth and equity [Ps 111:8]";[21] and the soul becomes clear-sighted, simplified, unified.[22] Meditation tends to produce

11. "Monastic Formation and Profession," *Rule of Benedict 1980*, ed. Timothy Fry, OSB (Collegeville, MN: Liturgical Press, 1981), 445ff.

12. Par 7; CF 55:91.

13. *Scala claustralium* and *Meditationes*; CS 48.

14. Guerric, Psalms 4.5; CF 32:77.

15. Bernard, 6pP 1.4; CF 53:121; John of Forde, S 13.10; CF 29:142.

16. Gilbert of Hoyland, S 29.3; CF 20:352; John of Forde, S 12.3; CF 29:223.

17. John of Forde, S 37.5; CF 43:99.

18. Gilbert of Hoyland, S 29.3; CF 20:280.

19. John of Forde, S 12.3; CF 29:219.

20. John of Forde, S 111.8; CF 47:139.

21. Baldwin of Forde, S 9.151; T 3; CF 38:93.

22. Isaac of Stella, S 12.6; CF 11:101.

love; it is a fire that "transforms and consumes within itself all the effort of the mind, so all that was meditation becomes wholly affection."[23] But it can also be a fruit of love: "Welcome indeed is the meditation that charity suggests."[24] For "who is fervent, if not one who meditates on the love of God?"[25]

Through the Middle Ages, *meditatio* remains closely linked with *ruminatio*. Saint Anselm graphically describes the process, at the same time giving new prominence to the elements of thinking and understanding:

> Consider again the strength of your salvation and where it is found. Meditate on it, delight in the contemplation of it. Taste the goodness of your Redeemer. Chew the honeycomb of his words, suck their flavor, which is sweeter than sap, swallow their wholesome sweetness. Chew by thinking, suck by understanding, swallow by loving and rejoicing.[26]

Gilbert of Hoyland is even more descriptive:

> Thanks be to you, Lord Jesus Christ, for making your sayings so sweet to my palate, surpassing honey in my mouth. So one mouthful, once tasted, scarcely leaves the tongue to be replaced by another. Slowly each morsel is masticated, or if it is swallowed whole, with a kind of gentle eructation it returns for rumination.[27]

Saint Bernard simply says in passing that his monks are familiar with the meaning of rumination: "You must become like clean ruminants."[28] He expects them to ruminate the psalms, and

23. Gilbert of Hoyland, Res div 5; CF 34:38.
24. Gilbert of Hoyland, SC 19.5; CF 20:244.
25. Bernard, Csi 5.31; CF 37:178.
26. *Meditatio redemptionis humanae* 8–11; *The Prayers and Meditations of Saint Anselm*, trans. Benedicta Ward (Harmondsworth: Penguin, 1973), 230. Hereafter Pr and Med.
27. S 5.1; CF 14:85.
28. OS 1.5; Luddy 3:335.

to find joy in doing so.[29] On Christmas Eve he exclaims: "Let us rejoice, ruminating within ourselves and repeating to each other the sweet words: 'Jesus Christ, the Son of God, is born in Bethlehem of Judah.'"[30]

This type of meditation extends beyond a simple repetition of a word or phrase to include other objects: the mysteries of Jesus—what Saint Bernard calls his "little bundle of myrrh"[31]— the wounds of Christ,[32] and his abundant goodness.

Since the subject matter for meditation is the Word of God as contained in the Scriptures, almost inevitably it leads to the writing of commentaries, which are both the fruit of meditation and an aid to those who wish to meditate. In the great commentaries of the Fathers, meditation and prayer well up spontaneously and are intertwined with the interpretation of the text. By a kind of organic development this tradition led to the medieval genre of meditations, among the first of which are those of John of Fécamp[33] and Saint Anselm of Canterbury[34] in the eleventh century. These works are already what William of Saint-Thierry calls *meditativae orationes*—meditations in the form of the faith, love, and devotion of the men who wrote them, of their intense longing for union with God, and of their consciousness of sin as they lay bare to the Lord their needs and aspirations. John of Fécamp's writings consist mainly of a tissue of quotations from the Bible and the Fathers, but constructed in a way that is entirely his own. Anselm's meditations are more theological, particularly the "Meditation on Human Redemption," which is a meditative summary of *Cur Deus Homo*, his theological treatise on the Atonement. His *Proslogion* and *Monologion* are also meant to be *exempli meditandi*. Anselm always "prayed his theology till there was no

29. Ben 10; Luddy 3:128; PP 2.2; Luddy 3:201; Div 16.7; SBOp 6A:149.
30. V Nat 6.2; Luddy 1:368.
31. SC 43.2-3; CF 7:221-2.
32. SC 62.7; CF 31:158; Gilbert of Hoyland, Redemp 6; CF 34:52.
33. *Jean de Fécamp, un maître de la vie spirituelle au XIe siècle*, trans. and ed. by Jean Leclercq and J. P. Bonnes (Paris: Vrin, 1946).
34. Pr and Med.

difference between theology and prayer";[35] thus he ends the "Meditation on Human Redemption":

> Lord, my heart is before you. I try, but by myself I can do nothing; do what I cannot. Admit me into the inner room of your love. I ask, I seek, I knock. You who made me seek, make me receive; you who gave the seeking, give the finding; you who taught the knocking, open to my knock.[36]

As in Anselm's meditations theology and prayer are wedded, the same is true in William of Saint-Thierry's *Meditativæ orationes*.[37] Although the title uses the plural form and the work was later divided by editors into twelve chapters or meditations, it is in reality a single sustained meditative prayer addressed to God throughout, and it is best approached as a single unit. Its unifying theme is William's desire and search for God. It is a search in which both his heart and his reason take part, "for his mysticism is always a 'rational' mysticism."[38] He "seeks [God's] love by means of understanding"[39] since "nothing is loved except by being understood nor understood except by being loved."[40]

At the beginning of the work, where William ponders the mystery of predestination, the rational element predominates. Toward the end, particularly in chapter twelve, the rational element returns. But already in chapter 2 the affective element comes to the fore as he begins to dwell on one of his favorite themes: the face of God. This image signifies for him all that is most intimate and divine in God, the innermost secret of his being. As he explains elsewhere, "To 'seek the face of God' is to seek knowledge of God face to face as Jacob saw God [Gen 32:30] . . . to see

35. Pr and Med 77.

36. 201-4; Pr and Med 237.

37. CF 3.

38. Jean Marie Déchanet, *William of St. Thierry: The Man and His Work*, trans. Richard Strachan, CS 10.

39. Med 12.11; CF 3:171.

40. Med 12.22; CF 3:175.

God as he truly is [1 John 3:2]."[41] Among William's favorite verses
from the psalms are those that speak of seeking God's face (Ps
26:8), the joy of God's face (Ps 15:11), walking in the light of God's
face (Ps 88:16), the face from which judgment comes forth (Ps
16:16:1), hiding in the secret of God's face (Ps 30:21), and the light
of God's face (Ps 4:7). If no one can see God and live (Exod 33:20),
William is even willing "to die that I may see, or see that I may
die."[42] For "to see God is faith's proper desire."[43]

Dwelling on this theme leads William to the heart of the
meditation (chapters 7, 8, and 11), where he gives full play to his
affections and pours out his deepest aspirations. Fulfillment of
these will only come at God's "self revelation to me, when I will
see what I love, and love with unperturbable joy what I see."[44]

As personal as the *Meditativæ orationes* is, underlying it are
the great mysteries of sin, human need, and Christ's redemption;
these themes have universal validity. William himself considered
his book to be "not without value for habituating the soul to the
search for God" in prayer,[45] it is also "an eloquent testimony to
his application to *lectio* and to his heart, full of desire and divine
contemplation."[46]

Whereas William is fascinated by the face of God, Ælred of
Rievaulx turns to the earthly Jesus. In the treatise *On Jesus at the
Age of Twelve (De Jesu puero duodenni)*,[47] Ælred meditates on a
single episode from the Gospel of Luke (2:41-50), exploring the
traditional senses of Scripture, historical, allegorical, and moral.
In the threefold meditation that is included as the third section
of his *Rule of Life for a Recluse (De Institutione inclusarum)*,[48] Ælred's
subject is the entire life of Christ as it unfolds in the gospels from

41. Ep frat 25; CF 12:18.
42. Med 3.1; CF 3.102.
43. Med 3.12; CF 3.107.
44. Med 12.20; CF 3.174.
45. Ep frat Preface 9; CF 12.6.
46. Bernardo Olivera, ocso, circular letter of January 26, 1993.
47. Iesu; CF 2.
48. Inst incl; CF 2.

the Annunciation to the Resurrection. These works are something "truly new and original. One finds nothing quite like them before him or among his contemporaries"[49]—and something that was to have a far-reaching influence in the later Middle Ages.[50] The recluse is instructed to enter into each scene with her whole self, especially with her senses and her imagination. She is to watch, to listen, to wonder. Each scene that Ælred depicts has its own special nuance for her devotion. He especially chooses scenes in which women take part; the recluse is to imitate and indeed to identify with them. It is interesting to note that, for Ælred also, a woman serves as a role model. In *On Jesus at Twelve*, after he has watched the sinner kiss the feet of Jesus, Ælred addresses his own soul: "What are you about, my soul, my wretched soul, my sinful soul? There certainly is the place for you safely to shed your tears, to atone for your impure kisses with holy kisses, to pour out all the ointment of your devotion free from fear."[51]

As the meditation in the *Rule of Life* continues, the recluse is to be more and more caught up in it. When Jesus is at table in Simon's house (Luke 7:36) and the sinful woman comes in, the recluse is to join her: "Together with that most blessed sinner approach his feet, wash them with your tears, wipe them with your hair, soothe them with kisses and warm them with ointments."[52] Then, when Mary of Bethany anoints the head of Jesus (Mark 14:3), the recluse must "Break the alabaster of your heart and whatever devotion you have, whatever love, whatever desire, whatever affection, pour it all out upon your Bridegroom's head."[53] At the Last Supper, when John reclines on the bosom of Jesus (John 13:25) and imbibes such sweetness, grace and tenderness, light and devotion from that fountain of mercy," the recluse

49. Charles Dumont, Introduction, *La vie de recluse*, SCh 76:27.

50. See Marsha L. Dutton, "The Cistercian Source: Ælred, Bonaventure, and Ignatius," *Goad and Nail: Studies in Cistercian History X*, ed. E. Rozanne Elder; CS 84.

51. Iesu 27; CF 2:34.

52. Inst incl 31; CF 2:83.

53. Inst incl 31; CF 2:85.

too is directed to "draw near and . . . not delay to claim . . . some portion of this sweetness."[54] She is to follow Christ throughout his Passion, compassionating with him, loving and adoring him. Their mystical union becomes most intense when blood and water come forth from his side (John 19:34). Ælred urges her to

> eat the honeycomb with your honey, drink your wine with your milk. The blood is changed into wine to gladden you, the water into milk to nourish you. From the rock streams have flowed for you, wounds have been made in his limbs, holes in the wall of his body, in which, like a dove, you may hide while you kiss them one by one.[55]

So much does she become one with Christ that "Your lips, stained with his blood, will become like a scarlet ribbon and your word sweet."[56]

Ælred then depicts the scenes of the deposition, the burial, and Mary Magdalen's encounter with Jesus on Easter morning. He ends with the holy women clasping the feet of Jesus, telling the recluse: "Linger here as long as you can."[57] He follows his meditation on the past with one on the present: the lives of a sinful and an innocent soul, as exemplified by himself and the sister to whom he is writing, and on the future: death, judgment, and beatitude. Present-day readers, however, may find, as medieval ones seem to have done, that it is the first part of this three-fold meditation that best makes "the sweet love of Jesus to grow in [their] affections."[58]

---

54. Inst incl 31; CF 2:87.
55. Inst incl 31; CF 2:90-1.
56. Inst incl 31; CF 2:91.
57. Inst incl 31; CF 2:92.
58. Inst incl 29; CF 2:79.

Chapter 4

STILLNESS

Quies, Requies, Otium, Sabbath, Vacare

"Teach us to care and not to care . . . teach us to sit still."[1]
All that is implied by "sitting still": withdrawal from everyday
activities, leisure, silence, a quiet mind and heart in order to enter
deeply into oneself and into the divine, denotes a state of being
held in great esteem even by the pre-Christian writers of antiquity.[2]
The words they used to describe it—*quies, otium, vacare*—were
taken over by the Christian tradition and given new orientation
and depth. To them were added the words *requies* and *Sabbath*.
Although these words are to some extent synonymous, each one
has its own nuances, so it is better to look at them separately.

QUIES

In classical Latin authors *quies* means rest, tranquillity; it is
opposed to what is in motion; it is related to the idea of security
and stability. There is also interior tranquillity [*quies animae*]. Seneca
gives the word a higher and more spiritual meaning. He sees the
love of *quies*, of leisure [*otium*], and peace, as virtues, opposed to
anger and uncontrolled passion. The way to a profound tranquillity
[*alta rerum quies*] is knowledge of God and of the destiny of man.[3]

Although in the Vulgate the word often simply means to cease
or to be quiet, there are a few passages where it has more profound

---

1. *T. S. Eliot, The Collected Poems and Plays* (New York: Harcourt, Brace and
World, n.d.), 67.
2. References in Jean Leclercq, *Otia Monastica* (Herder: Rome, 1963).
3. Seneca, *De clementis, De beneficiis, Dialogi.*

implications: Isaiah 30:15: "If you return and are quiet [*quiescatis*] you shall be saved; in silence and in hope shall your strength be"; Isaiah 66:1: "What is this house that you will build to me? And what is this place of my rest?" The First Letter of Peter (3:4) commends the incorruptibility of a quiet and a meek spirit. *Quies* is also used in that sense by Tertullian: an inner calm and attentiveness to God.[4] The early Fathers speak of the eternal rest [*aeternam quietam*] of the dead, the *quiescentes*.[5] The connection between *quies* and eschatology is magnificently developed by Saint Augustine, especially in his *City of God*: "All peace on earth is an anticipation of eternal peace";[6] "The vision of God will be peace and repose."[7]

If *quies* is a condition favorable for reflection and study, it is even more so for prayer, for being attentive to God. Thus it becomes associated with the lives of the early monks. Book 2 of the *Verba Seniorum* is entitled *De quiete*, translated from the Greek *hesychia*, which later becomes a very important technical term, and contains the apophthegma that would be so often quoted: "*Fuge, tace, quiesce:* these are the roots of not sinning."[8] "*Hesychia, quies,* is not merely a separation from noise and speaking with other people, but the possession of interior quiet and peace. . . . It means more specifically guarding the mind, constant remembrance of God, and the possession of inner prayer."[9]

In his *Rule*, Saint Benedict uses *quies* in the sense of 'to cease' (RB 44.8). More to the point, a monk who has been corrected is expected to be a peaceful [*quietus*] and obedient member of the community (RB 65.21).

The founders of Citeaux were in search of a place of *quies*. The word occurs several times in the *Exordium Parvum*, notably in chapter 2, the letter of Archbishop Hugh: "[they sought] to serve the Lord more advantageously and in greater quiet." Saint

---

4. De spectaculis, 15.2; CCSL 1:240.
5. Innocent I, *Epistola 25*; Celestine I, *Epistola 21*, for example.
6. Civ Dei 19.14; FC 24:231.
7. Civ Dei 22.29; FC 24:496.
8. *The Desert Fathers*, trans. Helen Wadell (New York: Vintage, 1998), 69.
9. Benedicta Ward, CS 59:xvi.

Bernard recognizes that in this life there is always an alternation between holy quiet [*sanctae quietis*] and necessary action;[10] but, adapting Paul's expression in the letter to the Philippians (1:23), he affirms that the better thing is to be, not dissolved, but still [*quiescere*] and with Christ.[11] He sees *quies* as the characteristic quality of wintertime, a stillness which will be present in heaven.[12] And, in spite of his fondness for images, he teaches that one must leave behind material images in order to be truly at rest, *quiescentem*. He gives a splendid description of the place of quiet, the room where "God is encountered not in angry guise nor distracted as it were by cares, but where his will is proved good and desirable and perfect . . . Here one may indeed be at rest. The God of peace pacifies all things, and to gaze on this stillness is to find repose [*quietum aspicere, quiescere est*]."[13]

Gilbert of Hoyland too speaks of the chamber of contemplation and repose [*contemplationis et quietis cubiculo*] where God is embraced.[14] He invites us to repose in the word of God; does Gilbert mean word or Word, or perhaps both?[15] But, paradoxically, he also says: "love is made more restless by love itself. Temptation rests, business rests, distress rests, but love knows not how to rest."[16]

REQUIES

Literally 'after-rest,' *requies* means rest or repose from labor, suffering, care. It is a word with especially rich biblical overtones. In biblical thought, rest is seen as the goal, beginning with God's rest after creation (Gen 2:2), in which Israel participates through the Sabbath (Exod 20:8-11). God promises his people rest (Exod

10. SC 51.1; CF 31:108.
11. SC 46.1; CF 7:240.
12. SC 33.6; CF 7:149.
13. SC 23.16; CF 7:40.
14. SC 13.7; CF 14:161.
15. SC 14.1; CF 14:166.
16. SC 2.6; CF 14:60-61.

30, 14), or threatens to withhold it (Ps 94:11; Heb 3:11, etc.). Rest is what Naomi seeks for her daughter-in-law (Ruth 3:1). Later, it is especially seeking wisdom which leads to rest (Sir 6:29; 51:27); so Jesus, Wisdom Incarnate, can promise rest to those who come to him (Matt 11:29). Finally, those who die in the Lord will find rest from their labors (Rev 14:13), a phrase which the Church incorporated into her liturgy for the dead: *requiem aeternam dona eis, Domine.* To distinguish the eternal rest of the Christian from that which the pagans meant by the same term, the Church added *requiescant in pace,* transposing the Sabbath rest of God after creation to that of the faithful after death.

For Saint Augustine, the human condition could be summed up in terms of *requies:* "You have made us for yourself, O Lord, and our hearts are restless until they rest in you."[17] Both Guerric of Igny's third Sermon for the Assumption of Mary[18] and Baldwin of Forde's fifth Tractate[19] are treatises on rest, commentaries on the same text, Sirach 24:11-13. Both stress the reciprocity of the rest: "Unless [the Son of Man] finds with us the rest he is seeking, we shall not find in him the rest we desire."[20] "For whom, then, has he sought rest? For himself, or for us? Or is it rather both for himself and for us? This is clearly the case";[21] "God is always stable and at rest,"[22] and by turning away from evil, the hearts of the faithful are prepared for Christ to rest in them.[23] In contrast "The godless person has to work even when he is resting."[24] For Baldwin, faith, hope, and charity prepare our hearts for Christ to rest in them. For Guerric, quoting Isaiah 66:2, it is especially humility:[25] "This rest will be achieved when God pleases us in

17. Conf 1.1; *Conf* 1/1:39.
18. CF 32:179ff.
19. CF 38:130ff.
20. Asspt 3; CF 32:182.
21. CF 38:131.
22. CF 38:131.
23. CF 38:135.
24. CF 32:180.
25. CF 32:183.

all things, and we displease God in nothing."[26] So Baldwin prays: "Lord God, you alone are the repose of souls . . . rest in me, that I may rest in you!"[27]

OTIUM

The general meaning of *otium* is given thus in the *Thesaurus Linguae Latinae:* "a) action is the chief thing negated, and then it means about the same as cessation from action, occupations, business . . . ; b) disturbance is the chief thing negated, and then it means quiet, security, tranquillity."[28] *Otium* thus lies midway between the two perils: *otiositas* and *negotium*, which is a very denial of *otium*. "*Otium*," writes Jean Leclercq, "is the major occupation of the monk. It is a very busy leisure: *negotiosissimum otium*, as Bernard and others have repeated."[29]

> In the course of the Latin Middle Ages, the specifically monastic kind of life is often designated by the terms: *quies, vacatio, sabbatum,* and especially *otium*. On the other hand, the monks are frequently warned against the dangers of *otium*. Obviously, the same term is used with very different meanings according to the immediate context. A deeper examination of the use of these terms, especially *otium*, reveals not only one of the essential aspects of the self-consciousness of medieval monasticism, but in addition its deep historical, intellectual and cultural roots in antiquity.[30]

The word *otium* had a long history in classical authors before it entered the Christian vocabulary. It is chiefly Seneca who uses the term *otium* in a way that presages the later Christian usage. By that term he means not only retirement from the world, quiet

26. CF 38:131.
27. CF 38:146.
28. *Thesaurus Linguae Latinae* (Leipzig: 1981) 9:1175-9.
29. Jean Leclercq, *The Love of Learning and the Desire for God: A Study of Monastic Culture,* trans. Catharine Misrahi (New York: Fordham UP, 1961), 84.
30. DSp (Paris: Letouzey et Ané, 1932–) 12:2746-56.

of soul [*quies animae*], and liberation from pleasures, but also application to the study of wisdom. He composed the first treatise, *De otio*. From him also comes the phrase which is taken up by William of Saint-Thierry and other medieval writers: rich leisure [*pingue otium*].

For *otium* is an ambiguous term. Besides *pingue otium*, there is another kind, a sterile kind: *otium iners*. This is not leisure, but idleness [*otiositas*], against which the Vulgate warns. "Idleness has taught much evil" (Sir 33:29); it leads to poverty and sin (Pr 12:11; 28:19; Ezek 16:49). We shall be held to account for every idle word (Matt 12:36). The workers in the market place are asked: "Why do you stand here all day idle?" (Matt 20:6).

The Fathers of the Church spontaneously repeat the use of *otium* current in their intellectual and social environment. *Otiosus* almost always has a negative meaning; *otium* often appears synonymous with *quies*; it has a certain kinship with *pax* and means both the mere cessation of activity, and leisure in view of intellectual work. Saint Augustine, in this differing from other Fathers, avoids using *otium* in a purely negative sense. He speaks of the "leisure of the Christian life,"[31] of being divinized in leisure [*deificari in otio*];[32] of leisure and rest [*otium et quies*].[33] The purpose of leisure is "the searching and finding of truth" and "the love of truth seeks holy leisure."[34] The monk's way of life is designated as *otium*; yet charity may require that those devoted to leisure should leave it to minister to the needs of others.[35]

In his use of the word, Augustine balances the two traditions of its meaning, philosophical and biblical, with equal fidelity to both. He is the first of the Fathers to emphasize the rare biblical passages in which *otium* has a positive meaning. This preoccupation produces his "neo-Platonic" exegesis of Psalm 45:11: "Be

31. Retrac 1.1; PL 32:585.
32. Epi 10; FC 81:75.
33. Epi 48.1; FC 12:231-2.
34. Civ Dei 19.19; FC 24:230.
35. Epi 48.2; FC 12232-3.

leisurely and you shall know that I am the Lord." He says: "Not
the leisure of idleness, but the leisure of thought so that it is free
from places and times. . . . The soul is therefore called to leisure,
so that it does not love those things which cannot be loved without labor."[36] Elsewhere he combines Psalm 45:11 with Sirach
38:25:

> Among those who know how to hear willingly and humbly
> and who lead a quiet life in sweet and healthful pursuits,
> let Holy Church be delighted, and let her say, "I am sleeping,
> and my heart keeps vigil (Sg 5:2)." What does it mean, "I
> am sleeping, and my heart keeps vigil," except, "I so rest
> that I may hear"? My leisure is not devoted to nurturing
> laziness but to gaining wisdom. "I am sleeping, and my
> heart keeps vigil." I am at leisure, and I see you are the Lord
> because "the wisdom of the scribe comes in his time of lei-
> sure, and he who is less in action shall gain it."[37]

In his *Rule*, Saint Benedict does not use the word *otium*, perhaps because of its negative connotations. He twice warns of idle
words in chapters 6.8 and 67.4, and even more forcefully of *otiositas*. The very first sentence of chapter 48, "On the Daily Manual
Labor," sums up his attitude: "Idleness [*otiositas*] is the enemy of
the soul." He especially warns against idleness during the time
of reading and on Sundays. This sense is taken by Benedict from
the *Regula Magistri* (50.1-7), which cites Proverbs 13:4 in this regard. The Benedictine tradition retains the same sense.

Saint Gregory the Great uses the term both in the positive
sense, *otio et vacatione*,[38] and in the negative sense.[39] Similarly,
Isidore of Seville says of *contemplationis otium*[40] "beware of idleness, do not love idleness, do not lead an idle life."[41] Cassiodorus,

---

36. Vera rel 35.65; CCSL 32:229-30.
37. In Ev Ioann 57.3; FC 90:16.
38. Hiez 2.7.5; Gray 223.
39. Mo 5.31.55; CCSL 143:256-8.
40. *De differentiis verborum* 2.34.132.
41. *Synonymorum* 2.18.19.

either directly or through Augustine, rejoins the classical tradition when he describes "the chief strength of the soul" as "when keeping away from every action, we repose in leisure, and with our bodily senses quiet, we treat something with greater depth and firmness."[42]

Paschasius makes *otium* a technical term for the monastic life. By alluding to Scipio's saying that he was never less idle than when he was idle, he explicitly assumes again the classical concept, but in addition he designates Christian *otium* as a happier *otium* and gives it priority. At the same time, he explains in what monastic *otium* consists: "meditating on sacred Scripture . . . on the traditions of the holy Fathers."[43]

This technical use of *otium* as meaning the monastic life is representative of that time and of the following centuries. Peter Damian speaks of the "salutary leisure" or "quiet" of the cloister.[44] This concept reaches its height in the twelfth century, particularly with the Benedictines and Cistercians. Peter the Venerable sees in the monks' busy leisure an anticipation of heavenly leisure. In the spirituality of Peter of Celles, *otium* and *quies* play such a capital role that his modern interpreter could entitle one chapter of his study "*Otium Quietis.*"[45] Moreover, the Benedictine concedes without jealousy: "True rest is in the Cistercian Order, where Martha is joined to Mary, where, according to the wise man's word, the active man should rest and the resting man should act."[46]

Bernard loves to play on the two meanings of *otium*: Malachy "passed without idleness [*otio*] the time he had given to leisure [*otio*];"[47] "idleness in leisure must be avoided."[48] Bernard also

---

42. *De anima* 6; CCSL 96:547-8.
43. *Expositio in Psalmi* 44.11.
44. *De contemptu sæculi* 29-30; PL 145:283-6.
45. Jean Leclercq, *La Spiritualite de Pierre de Celles* (Paris: 1946).
46. *Epistola 176*. Jean Leclercq describes those letters, discovered later, which are not in PL 202, in "Nouvelles lettres de Pierre de Celles," *Analecta Monastica 5, Studia Anselmiana 43* (Rome: Herder, 1958).
47. Mal 2.4; CF 10:110.
48. Csi 2.13.22; CF 37:76.

likes to juxtapose *otium* and *negotium*: "Does God's care of the world give way to the business—or rather the repose—of love [*negotia, immo otio, amoris*]? Yes, indeed."[49] "The leisure of wisdom is exertion [*sapientiae otia negotia sunt*], and the more leisure wisdom has, the harder it works in its own fashion."[50] One of the characteristics of a spouse-soul is the ability, in work and leisure alike, to keep God before her eyes.[51] Yet Bernard, like Augustine, realizes that charity may require one to withdraw from leisure: "Sweet as your leisure is charity does not fear to disturb it a little on her business."[52] He himself does not regret preferring the preparation of his sermons to his personal *otio* and *quieti*, provided his monks benefit from his admonitions.[53]

William of Saint-Thierry also contrasts the two kinds of *otium*: *pingue otium* and *otium iners*. The latter is "the greatest evil which can befall the mind," unemployed leisure. "Anyone who in his cell is not faithful and fervent in this activity is indeed idle."[54] On the other hand: "Is leisure to devote one's time to God idleness? Rather it is the activity of all activities [*negotium negotiorum*]."[55] He describes the bride of the Canticle "inactive in the idle busyness or busy idleness [*otioso negitio, sive negotioso otio*] of her little bed, all her actions and thought bent on this."[56]

Gilbert of Hoyland is also fond of the word *otium*, linking it with *quies, requies, sabbatum, vacare,* and particularly *libertas*: "What is more suited to the exercise of love than freedom and leisure?"[57] "The narrower the streets (Sg 3:2), the richer and more free is the interior leisure of the mind [*intus otia mentis*]."[58] He

49. SC 68.2; CF 40:18.
50. SC 85.8; CF 40:203.
51. SC 69.1; CF 40:27.
52. Ep 11.2; *Letters* 42.
53. SC 51.2; CF 31:42.
54. Ep frat 81-2; CF 12:39.
55. Ep frat 81; CF 12:39.
56. Cant 198; CF 6:159.
57. SC 5.6; CF 14:90.
58. Ibid.

makes a word play of his own: *"Quid otia dico? Devotionem dicerem justius."*[59]

SABBATH

It is perhaps significant that the Hebrew word "Sabbath" was not translated but simply taken over by Greek, Latin, and English. In the Old Testament it is expressly connected with a root meaning 'to desist,' 'to stop work.' It is a very ancient observance, intended for humanitarian purposes as a day of rest for human beings and animals (Exod 23:12; Deut 5:15), in imitation of God's rest after the six days of creation (Gen 2:2); but above all, it is for the worship of God. God calls it "a sign between myself and you . . . to show that it is I, the Lord, who sanctify you" (Exod 31:13). After the exile, observance of the Sabbath became one of the most fundamental principles of Judaism. However, by the time of Jesus, it was so encumbered with legal prescriptions that it had become a burden instead of a delight. In spite of this, Jewish tradition has managed to preserve the true character of the Sabbath, as can be seen from the explanation of a twentieth century rabbi: "What is the Sabbath? A reminder of every man's royalty; an abolition of the distinction between master and slave, rich and poor, success and failure . . . the Sabbath is holiness in time . . . the presence of eternity, a moment of majesty, the radiance of joy."[60]

For the early Christians, the Jewish Sabbath had been superseded by the Lord's day, the first day of the week. Yet they saw in the earthly Sabbath a foreshadowing of the eternal, heavenly one. In Augustine, this is expressed with particular eloquence: "This Sabbath will be perpetual. This rest will be ineffable; we cannot explain it—it is toward this that we tend, it was for this that we were reborn spiritually."[61] "Heaven will be the fulfillment of the Sabbath rest . . . the ultimate Sabbath [*maximum sabbatum*]

---

59. Ibid.

60. Abraham Heschel, "Sabbath," in *The World Treasury of Modern Religious Thought*, ed. Jaroslav Pelikan (Boston: Little, Brown, 1990), 559f.

61. S 362.27; *Sermons* III/10:263.

that has no evening, foreshadowed in the account of creation . . .
We ourselves will be like a seventh day when we shall be filled
with his blessing and remade by his sanctification."[62]

The Cistercians, with their medieval delight in making con-
nections, exploit the rich symbolism of the Sabbath as the seventh
day and the day of rest. For Gilbert of Hoyland, the sixth day is
both that of Christ's death and that of the soul's mystical death
to itself, and the seventh day is the Sabbath when Christ rested
in the tomb: "Laborious is the sixth day of your reformation, but
sweet are the Sabbaths of rest that follow."[63]

Adam of Perseigne speaks of the seven solemn festivals in
which the soul keeps itself from all servile work that it may be
free for God. Each festival is related to one of the gifts of the Holy
Spirit, and the seventh festival is the spirit of wisdom.[64] If each
of the festivals is in some sense a Sabbath, this one is the solemn
Sabbath of the Holy Spirit.[65]

It is Saint Ælred, in the *Mirror of Charity*, who develops this
symbolism most fully. Even under the Old Law, the Sabbath was
meant to leave the soul in a state of perfect openness to God,[66]
who is himself always at rest in his overflowing love, his everlasting and never changing Sabbath.[67] For Ælred, the six days of
creation correspond to six virtues: faith, hope, temperance, prudence, fortitude, and justice.[68] The seventh, characteristically, he
relates to charity, which brings perfect rest when the work of all
the virtues is completed.[69] Thus, those who love God find rest in
him, in that true calm and peace which is the Sabbath of the
soul.[70]

---

62. Civ Dei 22.30; FC 24:509-10.
63. SC 11.3; CF 14:145.
64. Ep 6; CF 21:114f.
65. Ep 9; CF 21:154.
66. Spec car 1.18.52; CF 17:116.
67. Spec car 1.19.56; CF 17:119.
68. Spec car 1.32.90-2; CF 17:142-4.
69. Spec car 1.33.93-7; CF 17 144-7.
70. Spec car 1.18.52; CF 17:116.

In the third part of the Mirror, Ælred expands the symbolism to include three Sabbaths: the first, that of the seventh day; the second, that of the seventh year (Lev 25:1-7); the third, that of the fiftieth or jubilee year (Lev 25:8-17), the Sabbath of Sabbaths. These correspond to the three objects of the command to love: our self, our neighbor, and God.[71] First comes peace within oneself: "the seventh day of rest made possible by six days of labor in good works . . . the day we put aside servile works, forebearing to light the fire of lust, and casting down the burden of our passions."[72] Then, peace with others: "We must gather all the world to our hearts to share in our peace."[73] As a year is made up of many days, this sabbatical year is a "welding together of many souls and many hearts into one, in the fire of charity"— from family and friends to enemies.[74] Lastly, peace with God: "we gaze on the One who is forever changeless, and as we gaze thereon, we are perfectly at rest. So great is the delight we find in God's embrace that this is indeed the Sabbath of all Sabbaths."[75] "Let us know him alone, and enjoy him alone, and being always one in him, we shall always be at rest in him, celebrating our perpetual Sabbath."[76]

VACARE, VACATIO

The basic meaning is 'to be unoccupied, to have leisure or time, to be free from occupation.' Characteristic uses that would be much quoted and exploited by later authors are Psalm 45:11; *vacare et videte*, "be still and know, see, that I am God," and Sirach 38:25: "The wisdom of a scribe comes by his time of leisure" (*in vacuitatis tempore*). With an object in the dative case, it means 'to be free for, to give oneself to;' and the quality of the *vacatio* depends

71. Spec car 3.1.1; CF 17:221.
72. Spec car 3.3.6; CF 17:225.
73. Spec car 3.4.7; CF 17:226.
74. Spec car 3.4.8; CF 17:227.
75. Spec car 3.6.17; CF 17:232.
76. Spec car 3.1.1; CF 17:221.

on the object. Thus in Tobit 6:18, Raphael's advice to Tobias is that for the first three days of their marriage, he and Sarah should give themselves to prayers: *nihil aliud nisi orationibus vacabis cum ea.* The same expression, and the same object—in order to pray—are used by Paul in 1 Corinthians 7:5. This is the sense it continued to have in early Christian literature. The proper objects of *vacare* are God and Christ, worship and *lectio.*

Augustine contrasts *inanis vacatio* with the *fructuosa vacatio* of those who know and understand the mystery of Christ. In the *City of God*, he explores the great mystery of God's Sabbath rest after the six days of creation [*Dei vacatio*],[77] the rest which signifies the repose of those who rest in him, and of whose rest God is the cause.[78]

Benedict knows *vacare* in both a good and a bad sense. Its proper object is *lectio*, and he is at pains to allow considerable time for that in his *horarium.* Unoccupied time not directed to this object easily becomes the wrong kind of *vacatio*, as in RB 48.18, 23, and idleness which is apt to be filled with idle talk (43.8). Later on, *soli Deo vacare* becomes almost a technical term for the eremitical life and is applied to someone who becomes a hermit.

For Bernard, the proper objects of *vacare* are God, or the divine praises,[79] or, interestingly, the beauty of God [*vacare et videre quoniam speciosus est Deus*].[80] In his second Sermon for the Assumption, taking his cue from the Gospel parable of the house that is swept, garnished, and empty (Matt 12:44), Bernard describes the sweeping, accomplished by the regular observance, which is the role of Martha. Then playing on the meaning of *vacans*, he describes Mary's role as that of filling the house: "her time is left vacant to attend to the Lord so that the house itself may not be left vacant by him [*vacat (Maria) enim Domino, ut non*

77. Civ Dei 11.6; FC 14:196.
78. Civ Dei 11.8; FC 14:198-9.
79. SC 10.9; CF 4:66.
80. SC 22.3; CF 7:16.

sit domus vacans]."[81] "*Tibi vaco,*" William of Saint-Thierry advises, "Give your attention to yourself," but this is only a preparation for the activity par excellence [*negotium negotiorum*],[82] the proper activity of solitaries: *vacare Deo, frui Deo.*[83]

Gilbert of Hoyland places *vacatio* between investigation [*vestigatio*] and the vision of wisdom. But even if given second place, it is a prerequisite for the other two. For without it, truth can neither be investigated nor, if it is found, can it be envisioned.[84] Commenting on Isaiah 58:13, Gilbert says: "The Sabbath is the delightful and holy and glorious day of the Lord." He distinguishes three degrees of *vacatio*: "If you are free [*si vacans*], you have a Sabbath; if you are free and have eyes [*si vacas et vides*] (Ps 45:11) to contemplate the delights of the Lord, then your Sabbath is delightful and holy; but a glorious Sabbath of the Lord, a Sabbath within a Sabbath, is freedom in freedom [*vacatio de vacatione*]."[85]

81. Asspt 2.7; Luddy 3:232.
82. Ep frat 104; CF 12:46.
83. Ep frat 81; CF 12:39.
84. SC 36.4; CF 26:439.
85. SC 11.5; CF 14:145.

Chapter 5

MERCY WITHIN MERCY

Misericordia and *Miseria*

As Thomas Merton made his rounds as fire watchman on the night of July 4, 1952, "a voice [was] heard in Paradise: 'Have you had sight of me, Jonas my child? Mercy within mercy within mercy.'"[1] In singling out mercy as God's all-embracing quality, Merton is echoing a conviction that runs throughout the Judeo-Christian tradition, reaching back to Israel's encounter with YHWH on Mount Sinai, when he himself proclaimed: "The Lord, the Lord, a God of tenderness and compassion, slow to anger and rich in mercy" (Exod 34:6). God is love, indeed (1 John 4:8), but mercy is the special kind of love that the sinfulness of fallen humanity calls forth in him, and it is precisely after Israel's apostasy when the people "turned aside from the way [God] had pointed out for them, making for themselves a molten calf and worshiping it" (Exod 32:8) that he reveals himself as mercy.

Mercy, in Hebrew *chesed*, as the most comprehensive description of Israel's God, is taken up by the psalms and the prophets (Jonah 4:2; Joel 2:13). This mercy is faithful, *emeth*: it continues for a thousand generations, and the two words will be used throughout the Hebrew Scriptures. If God also tells Moses: "I will have mercy on whom I will have mercy, and I shall show pity to whom I shall show pity" (Exod 33:19), this does not imply any limits to it, but simply underlines how utterly free and gratuitous it is.[2]

---

1. *The Sign of Jonas* (New York: Harcourt, Brace, 1953), 362.
2. Theodore Koehler (DSp 10:1317) points out that the parallelism of Exod

The psalms, especially toward the end of the Psalter, lay great emphasis on the proclamation or confession of God's mercy and fidelity (Ps 99:5; 102:17; 105:1; 106:1; 117:2), reaching a climax in Psalm 135, a veritable litany of God's mercies. "All God's ways are mercy and faithfulness" (Ps 24:10; 35:6; 39:11; 56:4; 60:8; 83:12; 84:11; 87:12; 88:2, 25, 34; 97:3). It follows that this mercy is everlasting. The psalmist will sing of it forever (Ps 88:2); the earth is full of the mercy of God (Ps 32:5; 118:64).

The Israelites are therefore confident that they can rely on YHWH's mercy, and the psalms abound in pleas for mercy, especially in the early part of the Psalter (Ps 6:2; 24:16; 25:11; 26:7; 30:10; 40:5; 50:3; 56:2). Different reasons are given to persuade God to have mercy; most frequently, because the petitioner is poor, needy, sick (Ps 6:2; 30:10, etc.), above all because the petitioner has sinned (Ps 40:5). Other reasons include: "because I trust in you" (Ps 56:2); "because I have loved your commandments" (Ps 118:159); "because I cry to you all day long" (Ps 85:3); or simply "because of your great mercy" (Ps 50:3). Mercy is better than life (Ps 62:4); it is truly a name for God: "My God, my Mercy" (Ps 58:18; 143:2).

If faithfulness goes with mercy, so, too, do justice and hope: "I am the Lord who exercises mercy and judgment and justice in the land" (Jer 9:24); Sirach advises those "who fear the Lord to wait for his mercy . . . hope in him, and mercy will come to you" (Sir 2:7-9).

There is indeed another side to God, seemingly opposed to his mercy: his wrath. But the two qualities are not on an equal plane. Even though God, provoked by Israel's ever recurring infidelities, cries out: "I will not spare, and I will not pardon, nor will I have mercy" (Jer 13:14; 16:5; Ezek 5:11; 7:4; 9:10), Israel is confident that "His wrath will come to an end; he will not be angry for ever" (Ps 102:9), and indeed, this proves to be the case. Nowhere is this more passionately portrayed than in Hosea,

---

33:19: mercy/mercy, show pity/show pity, makes it a paraphrase of Exod 3:14, "I am who I am": thus the name of YHWH is *mercy.*

where the Lord himself cries out: "How could I give you up, O Ephraim, or deliver you up, O Israel? . . . My heart is overwhelmed, my pity is stirred. I will not give vent to my blazing anger" (Hos 11:8-9). "For a short moment I forsook you," the Lord tells Israel in the prophecy of Isaiah, "but with great mercies will I gather you. In a moment of indignation I hid my face from you a little while, but with everlasting kindness have I had mercy on you, says the Lord your Redeemer" (Isa 54:7-8). "Though I struck you in my wrath, yet in my good will I have shown you mercy" (Isa 60:10).

Musing on the greatness of God's mercy (Sir 2:23), Sirach nevertheless warns against presuming on it: "Say not, 'the mercy of the Most High is great, and he will have mercy on the multitude of my sins,' for mercy and wrath quickly come from him" (Sir 5:6-7; 16:12-13). It is because humans are short-lived that God "pours forth his mercy on them" (Sir 18:9). "The compassion of man is towards his neighbor, but the mercy of God is upon all flesh. He has mercy, and teaches, and corrects, as a shepherd does his flock. He has mercy on him who receives the discipline [*doctrinam*] of mercy" (Sir 18:12-14). Confidently, then, Sirach can turn to pray for his people: "Have mercy upon us, O God of all, and behold us, and show us the light of your mercies" (Sir 31:1; 36:14-15).

The author of the book of Wisdom links God's mercy with his omnipotence: "You have mercy on all, because you can do all things" (Wis 11:24), and his providence: "But you, our God, are gracious and true, patient, and ordering all things in mercy" (Wis 15:1). He is Lord of mercy (Wis 9:1); his mercy is given to the little ones (Wis 6:7) and to his holy ones (Wis 4:15), but "as to the wicked . . . there came upon them wrath without mercy" (Wis 19:1).

Mercy is a human quality as well as a divine one: the just person "shows mercy and lends all the day long" (Ps 36:26); "He is merciful, compassionate, and just" (Ps 111:4). This is stressed in the Wisdom books. Mercy is its own reward—a merciful person does good to his own soul (Prov 11:17; 22:9). One who has mercy on the poor lends to the Lord (Prov 19:19), and is forgiven his iniquity (Prov 16:6). The wicked person, on the other hand, will not have mercy on his neighbor (Prov 21:10); for anger has no mercy (Prov 27:4). In order to receive mercy, one must show it: "In judging, be merciful to the fatherless . . . and you shall be as the obedient son of the Most High, and he will have mercy on you more than a mother" (Sir 4:10-11). For if one "has no mercy on a man like himself, does he entreat mercy [from the Lord] for his own sins?" (Sir 28:4) However, in order to please God, one's own soul must be the first object of one's mercy (Sir 30:24).

With mercy go truth and justice (Prov 3:3; 20:28; 21:3, 21). "Sow for yourselves in justice, and reap in the mouth of mercy" (Hos 10:12); "What does the Lord require of you but to do justice and love mercy and walk solicitous with your God" (Mic 6:8); "Judge true judgment and show mercy and compassion" (Zech 7:9).

The reverse side of mercy, as it were, is misery, and it is in the book of Job that we find the misery of human life expressed most poignantly. "Why," Job demands, "is light given to him that is in misery, and life to those who are in bitterness of soul?" (Job 3:20) Already filled with affliction and misery (Job 10:15), he anticipates only going "to a land that is dark and covered with the mist of death, a land of misery and darkness" (Job 11:20-22). He implores his friends: "Have pity on me, have pity on me, at least you my friends, for the hand of the Lord has touched me" (Job 19:21). This is all the more grievous, since it was God who had formed him and granted him life and mercy (Job 10:12); indeed, he tells us, "From my infancy, mercy grew up with me" (Job 31:18).

* * *

To the cry that resounds throughout the Old Testament: "Show us, O Lord, your mercy" (Ps 84:8), God responds with divine munificence by sending his merciful love incarnate in Jesus of Nazareth. No wonder that people cry out to him for mercy: the blind (Matt 9:27; 20:30), the Canaanite woman (Matt 15:22), the father of the possessed boy (Matt 17:14). It is a cry that the Church will echo through the ages: *Kyrie eleison!* The heart of Jesus could not but be moved to pity by human need and misery; the gospels underline this particularly in the case of lepers (Mark 1:41; Luke 17:13), the widow of Naim (Luke 7:13), and the crowds of people "troubled and abandoned, like sheep without a shepherd" (Matt 9:36). Mary and Zachary sing of God's mercy in their canticles: it was promised to their ancestors (Luke 1:55, 72), and it endures from age to age for those who fear him (Luke 1:50). For Zachary it is the mercy which comes from the *splagchna*, the innermost heart of God (Luke 1:78). The tax collector is justified by his prayer: "O God, be merciful to me a sinner" (Luke 18:13), and though the word is not used, the father of the prodigal is an icon of the heavenly Father's mercy (Luke 15:11-32). Jesus expects his followers to be merciful, as their heavenly Father is (Luke 6:36), for then they too will obtain mercy (Matt 5:7); he illustrates this by the parable of the good Samaritan. (Luke 10:30-37) On the other hand, the unmerciful servant will receive punishment rather than mercy from his master (Matt 18:23-34).

Although the Johannine vocabulary does not include "mercy"—*agape* has taken its place—the Prologue of John's gospel speaks of seeing in the Word made flesh the glory of God, "full of grace and truth," *charis* and *aletheia*, recalling the Hebrew *chesed* and *emeth*, as does the Letter to the Hebrews in calling Jesus a "merciful and faithful high priest" (Heb 2:17). For Paul it is *agape* and *charis*, "grace" which best express the idea of God's mercy. In Ephesians (4:32) and Colossians (3:12), mercy is among the virtues the Christian should practice. Paul's most extensive use of "mercy" is in Romans 9–11, when he is wrestling with the place of the Jews in God's plan, working with quotations from the Scriptures, especially Exodus 33:19 and Hosea. He concludes his argument by explaining that God shut up all, both Jews and Gentiles, in disobedience, that he might have mercy on all (Rom 11:32). Perhaps this is what led him to make his appeal to the Romans "by the mercies of God" (Rom 12:1). Later on in the letter he cites the familiar pair, *chesed* and *emeth*, to explain the different motives for Jewish and Gentile Christians to be grateful to God: the Gentiles for God's mercy, the Jews for his faithfulness (Rom 15:8-9).

* * *

The Latin word *misericordia*, used in the Vulgate to translate *chesed*, adds its own significant nuance. "The Vulgate," Merton observes, "rings with *misericordia* as though with a deep church bell. Mercy is the 'burden' or the 'bourdon,' it is the bass bell and undersong of the whole Bible."[3] Saint Augustine points out that mercy "gets its Latin name *misericordia*, from the sorrow of someone who is miserable; it is made up of two words, *miser*, miserable, and *cor*, heart. It means being heartsore. So when someone else's misery or sorrow touches and pierces your heart, it's called *misericordia*, or soreness of heart."[4] Elsewhere he says: "*Misericordia* is so called because it makes *miserum* the heart, *cor*, of someone who feels compassion for another's misfortune."[5] No wonder the Latin writers, beginning with Augustine himself, exploit the possibilities of the antithesis *miseria/misericordia*.

If this antithesis is so significant to Augustine, it is because he is so aware of both his own misery and the mercy God has shown him. This is an underlying theme of his *Confessions*. God is the "merciful God," "most merciful, [*misericordissima*][6] indeed "the fount of mercy,"[7] and Augustine "your miserable suppliant."[8] "Allow me," he prays, "to speak in your merciful presence, for it is to your mercy that I address myself."[9] Looking back, he sees God's mercy at work at every stage of his life: "At

3. *Seasons of Celebration* (New York: Farrar, Straus and Giroux, 1956), 175; hereafter, Seasons.

4. S 358A.1; *Sermons* 3/10:196.

5. Mor eccl cath 27.53; PL 32:1333.

6. Conf 6.5.7; *Conf* 141; Conf 6.9.13; *Conf* :146

7. *Conf* 4.4.7; *Conf*: 97; Conf 6.1.1; *Conf* 135; Conf 6.16.26; *Conf* 156.

8. 1.6.9; *Conf* 44.

9. 1.6.7; *Conf* 42-3.

my birth I was welcomed by the tender care your mercy provided for me."[10] In his turbulent adolescence, "far above me your faithful mercy was hovering."[11] "You began little by little to work on my heart with your most gentle and merciful hand."[12] "By your merciful providence [my] worldly behavior always brought bitter disappointments."[13]

There is a false kind of mercy, to which Augustine was prone in his youth, and which he describes at some length in Book 3: "Someone is moved by watching scenes on stage, although his state of mind is usually called misery when he is undergoing them himself and mercy when he shows compassion for others so afflicted."[14] "It is possible to enjoy sad feelings; yet there can be no doubt that everyone aspires to be happy. Can this be the reason: no one wants to be miserable, but we do like to think ourselves merciful."[15] Yet though he could weep for Dido, he had no tears for himself; and "What indeed is more pitiful than a piteous person who has no pity for himself? *Quid enim miserius misero non miserante se ipsum?*"[16]

The death of a dear friend was the occasion of more genuine feelings of misery: "I was beset with misery and bereft of my joy *miser eram et amiseriam gaudium meum.*"[17] "The mute sufferings of my mind reached your mercy as loud cries."[18] "As I grew more and more miserable, you were drawing near."[19]

At the height of his struggles, "this deep meditation dredged all my wretchedness up from the secret profundity of my being and heaped it all together before the eyes of my heart. . . . I ut-

10. 1.6.7; *Conf* 42-3.
11. 3.3.5; *Conf* 78.
12. 6.5.7; *Conf* 141.
13. 6.10.17; *Conf* 150.
14. 3.2.2; *Conf* 76.
15. 3.2.3; *Conf* 76.
16. 1.13.21; *Conf* 53.
17. 4.5.10; *Conf* 98.
18. 7.7.11; *Conf* 168.
19. 6.15.25; *Conf* 156.

tered cries of misery."[20] "In my secret heart you stood by me, Lord, redoubling the lashes of fear and shame in the severity of your mercy,"[21] until finally the Lord who is "good and merciful . . . plumbed the depths of my death, draining the cesspit of corruption in my heart, so that I ceased to will all that I had been wont to will, and now willed what you willed" (Matt 26:39).[22]

Writing years after the experience, he admits: "You are merciful, I in need of mercy."[23] Indeed, "my life is full of weaknesses, and my sole hope is your exceedingly great mercy."[24]

The antithesis misery/mercy occurs in many other of Augustine's writings, especially his sermons on the psalms. "'Have mercy on me, God, according to your great mercy' (Ps 50:3). A person who is driven to beg for great mercy is confessing great misery."[25] There is no more poignant instance than when he is describing the scene when those who had accused the woman taken in adultery (John 8:9) have gone away: "The two were left alone, Misery and Mercy."[26]

Augustine points out how often mercy is linked with truth or faithfulness in the Scriptures. "'All the Lord's ways are steadfast love and truth' (Ps 24:10). Mercy? How is he merciful? In forgiving sins. And truth? Yes, because he keeps his promises."[27] He also links mercy with justice or judgment. "'He loves mercy and judgment,' (Ps 100:1) accept his mercy and fear his judgment."[28] "At present his mercy is preached to you, but later his justice will be manifested, for God is not merciful in such a

20. 8.12.28; *Conf* 205-6.

21. 8.11.25; *Conf* 204.

22. 9.1.1; *Conf* 209.

23. 10.28.39; *Conf* 262.

24. 10.35.57; *Conf* 275; 0.29.40; *Conf* 263; 10.32.48; *Conf* 269; 10.36.58; *Conf* 275.

25. En in Ps 50.6; *Psalms* 3/16:414; En in Ps 56.17; *Psalms* 3/16:118; En in Ps 118(5):3; *Psalms* 33/19:361.

26. In Ev Joann 33.5.4; FC 88:56.

27. En in Ps 68(1).17; *Psalms* 3/17:381; En in Ps 60.9; *Psalms* 3/17:200; En in Ps 88(1).1; *Psalms* 3/18:273; En in Ps 97.2; *Psalms* 3/18:460.

28. En in Ps 32(1).2; *Psalms* 3/15:407.

way as to be unjust, nor just in such a way as to leave no room
for mercy. . . . If you have spurned God's mercy you will feel
his justice; but if you have not spurned his mercy, his justice will
be your joy."[29] God's judgment is not in opposition to his mercy:
"Do you want to hear what the Lord's mercy is like? Give up
your sins, and he will forgive your sins. And do you want to hear
about his justice? Hold fast to righteousness, and your righteousness will be crowned."[30] Nevertheless, as Edmund Hill points
out, "The contrast between mercy and justice is a decidedly
Roman idea, quite foreign to the Israelite or biblical way of thinking. There, justice includes mercy, and this is particularly true of
God's justice, which is not merely a matter of a quid pro quo and
tit for tat, but of 'doing the right thing.'"[31]

The way to assure God's mercy toward us, Augustine
teaches, is to show mercy toward others:

> The Lord God is merciful and compassionate and just. We
> love to think of how merciful and compassionate he is, but
> perhaps we are terrified when we remember that the Lord
> God is just. Do not fear, do not despair, you blessed one,
> you who fear the Lord and are full of good will about his
> commands; simply be kind, be merciful and lend (Ps
> 111:5). . . .When you forgive that you may be in turn for-
> given (Lk 6:37), you are showing mercy. . . In a general
> sense any action designed to relieve another's misery can
> be called mercy.[32]

Commentating on the psalm verse: "His mercy is eternal,"
(Ps 135:1), Augustine explains how the psalmist can call God's
mercy eternal:

> After the judgment that will take place at the end of the age
> . . . there will not be anyone thereafter upon whom God

29. En in Ps 39.19; *Psalms* 3/16:213-4.
30. En in Ps 39.19; *Psalms* 3/16:213-14.
31. S 144, n.5; *Sermons*, 3/4:434.
32. En in Ps 111.4; *Psalms*, 3/19:294.

can exercise his mercy. All the same, there is a way in which we can speak correctly of God pouring out his mercy for all eternity on his holy, faithful servants, not in the sense that they will be miserable for ever and therefore eternally in need of his mercy but because there will never be an end to the happiness he mercifully grants to the miserable, thus changing their misery into beatitude.[33]

One can hear Augustine identifying with the psalmist who cried out: "My God, my mercy" (Ps 58:18). "Filled as [the psalmist] was with the good gifts of God, what else could he call his God, except 'his mercy'? And what a name this is, a name for everyone to shelter under, to escape from despair! . . . All that I am, absolutely everything that I am, comes from your mercy."[34]

* * *

Pope Saint Leo speaks frequently of God's ineffable mercy, shown in the Incarnation,[35] "a mystery that involves such great mercy,"[36] when [divine] wrath was converted into mercy.[37] "The Father and the Son had one will and one plan . . . mercifully established and unchangeably fixed before the eternal ages."[38] So Leo urges his people, "Let us flee to the mercy of God,"[39] for to no one does he deny it.[40]

The mysteries of divine mercy all converge in the paschal mystery.[41] "His mercy underwent the sufferings of our mortality, that he might save it."[42] Indeed, "He who came to save sinners

33. En in Ps 135.1; *Psalms* 3/20:214.
34. En in Ps 58(2).11; *Psalms* 3/17:176.
35. S 33.2; FC 93:139.
36. S 29.1; FC 93:121.
37. S 33.1:3; FC 93:139.
38. S 58.4:2; FC 93:252.
39. S 43.4; FC 93:189.
40. S 35.4; FC 93:153.
41. S 49.4; FC 93:212.
42. S 58.4:2; FC 93:252; S 21.3; FC 93:79.

(1 Tim 1:15) did not deny his mercy even to his own murderers"[43] (Luke 23:44).

Since we have received such great mercy, Leo stresses our need to show it to others, that "by having mercy on God's poor we might deserve his mercy."[44] For "what hope remains for sinners who do not even show mercy for the sake of obtaining it themselves?"[45] (Matt 5:7) Even those who are "full of faith, chaste, sober, and adorned with other noteworthy habits, if they are not merciful, do not deserve mercy."[46] Even justice is not enough: "How indeed will your justice be richer that of the scribes and Pharisees (Matt 5:20) unless [your] mercy is even more so?"[47] (Jas 2:13) God is not only Justice, he is Mercy, and "Mercy wants you to be merciful."[48]

While Leo speaks often of almsgiving as an expression of mercy,[49] it also includes pardoning offenses.[50] Fasting and mercy should go together,[51] and all should be done with a cheerful spirit: "Let works of mercy be our delight."[52]

* * *

It is surprising that in his *Rule*, Saint Benedict uses *misericordia* so seldom: six times in all. Mercy is to be shown to the brother who needs more (RB 34.4), but he is not to take pride in it; Benedict expects that human nature itself will show mercy to the young and the elderly (RB 37.1); the abbot is exhorted to be merciful, that he too may win mercy (RB 64.10). Perhaps Bene-

43. S 67.3: FC 93:292.
44. S 17.1; FC 93:64.
45. S 11.1; FC 93:47.
46. S 10.2; FC 93:44.
47. S 92.1:2; FC 93:386.
48. S 95.7; FC 93:398.
49. S 7.1; FC 93:36; S 13; FC 93:54; S 44.2.2; FC 93:191, etc.
50. S 48.4; 178; FC 93:208: S 49.5; FC 93:213.
51. S 81.4; FC 93:351, etc.
52. S 40.4; FC 93:174.

dict's most significant use of mercy is the very first one; in chapter 4, "Never to despair of God's mercy," (RB 4:74) is the last of the seventy-four "instruments of good works." If Benedict begins his list with our love of God (RB 4.1), it is God's merciful love for us which will sustain us and bring us to our goal.

* * *

Saint Gregory the Great sees that the all powerful God is also merciful.[53] "In this appears all the mercy of the heart [*viscera*] of almighty God: seeing men depart from him, he seeks to bring them back."[54] God's merciful heart [*gremium*] is open to us,[55] and Gregory is enraptured by that thought:

> What tongue can describe the heart *viscera* of the divine mercy? What mind is not amazed by the riches of such great love? The psalmist was thinking of these riches of divine love when he said: "My helper, I will sing a psalm to you. It is you, O God, who are my protector, my God, my mercy." (Ps 58:18) . . . He could not just speak of God as being merciful but called him mercy itself, saying: "My God, my mercy."[56]

God's mercy was shown especially in the Incarnation: "When [the Lord] had been made man he had mercy on human misery."[57] "Our Redeemer's mercy has mitigated for us the rigor of the Law. . . He mercifully set free those it justly condemned."[58] Commenting on Christ's words "You are my friends," (John 15:14) Gregory exclaims: "How great is our Creator's mercy! We were unworthy servants, and he calls us friends."[59] When the sinful woman (Luke 7:36) "ran to the fountain of mercy to be washed

53. Mor 13.32.36; SCh 212:294; Mor 15.53.60; SCh 221:106.
54. Mor 16:58:71; SCh 221:246.
55. Hom in ev 33.8; CS 76:278.
56. Hom in ev 19.7; CS 123:85.
57. Mor 5.34.63; PL 75:714.
58. Hom in ev 33.8; CS 123:276.
59. Hom in ev 27.3; CS 123:214.

clean . . . [Jesus] drew her inwardly by his mercy, and received
her outwardly by his gentleness."[60]

* * *

Saint Anselm, puzzling over the mystery of why God became man, gives a negative answer to the question "Whether it
is fitting to forgive a sin out of mercy alone, without any restitu-
tion of what is owed to him,[61] even if man cannot make
repayment."[62] "Mercy of this kind is absolutely contrary to God's
justice. Yet God is merciful"[63] (Ps 35:7-8). "How, then," Boso asks,
"will man be saved, if he does not himself pay what he owes,
and is bound not to be saved if he does not pay?" "What effron-
tery it is on our part," Anselm replies, "to assert that God, who
is rich in mercy (Eph 2:4) beyond human understanding, cannot
do this merciful thing?"[64] Indeed, he can:

> How great and just the mercy of God is. The mercy of God
> which, when we were considering the justice of God and the
> sin of mankind, seemed to you to be dead (1:25), we have
> found to be so great, and so consonant with justice, that a
> greater and juster mercy cannot be imagined. What, indeed,
> can be conceived of more merciful than that God the Father
> should say to a sinner condemned to eternal torments and
> lacking any means of redeeming himself, "Take my only-
> begotten Son and give him on your behalf", and that the Son
> himself should say, "Take me and redeem yourself."[65]

But it is in his prayers and meditations that Anselm uses
mercy and misery most often. Whether he prays to Mary, John

60. Hom in ev 33.1; CS 76:269; Hom in ev 34.2; CS 123:281.
61. Cur 1.12; *Anselm of Canterbury, the Major Works* (Oxford: OUP, 1998), 284
(henceforth MW).
62. Cur 1.24; MW 311.
63. Cur 1.24: MW 312.
64. Cur 1.25; MW 313.
65. Cur 2.20; MW 354.

the Baptist, Peter, Paul, or any other saint, it is always for mercy that he prays, conscious of his misery. He is "the most wretched of wretches, *miserrime miserum.*"[66] Typical is this prayer:

> See, here is a soul needing mercy, and here is the merciful apostle Peter before the God of mercy, who had mercy upon the apostle Peter . . . . See, here is misery, and there is mercy: the mercy of God and his apostle Peter, and a soul in misery.[67]

* * *

This juxtaposition of misery and mercy is at the heart of the early Cistercians' teaching. Saint Bernard links them explicitly: "It is mercy, not misery, that makes a person happy, but *miseria* is the home of *misericordia,*"[68] as does William of Saint-Thierry: "My [God's] will is that my mercy would be very near the miserable."[69] It is this conviction that enables the Cistercians to look deeply into the miseries of our fallen nature, both in themselves,[70] and in the whole human race, without pessimism. "Truly, we are altogether miserable!" cries Baldwin of Forde. "We were born in misery; we have been raised in misery to this very moment; henceforth we will live in misery; and at last in misery we will die! Inside ourselves we are full of misery, and outside ourselves misery surrounds us."[71] Bernard enumerates the miseries of his own soul: it is "burdened with sins, enveloped in darkness, enslaved to pleasure, tormented with desires, dominated by passions, filled with delusions, always prone to evil, easily

66. Orat 9; *The Prayers and Meditations of Saint* Anselm, trans. Benedicta Ward (Harmsworth; Penguin, 1973), 135.

67. Ibid., 139.

68. Conv 12; CF 25:46.

69. Med 1;10; CF 3:93.

70. William, Med 9.1; CF 3:145; Ælred, Iesu 1.1; CF 2:3; Orat past 3; CF 2:107; John of Forde, S 21.5; CF 39:96-7.

71. S 17.8-9; CF 41:50.

accessible to every vice, in a word, full of all shame and confusion,"[72] and describes the strange human paradox:

> The soul, in a strange and evil way, is both held as a slave in this voluntary and yet irresistible bondage, and it is free. It is enslaved and free at the same time; enslaved through bondage, free because of its will, and, which is even stranger and more unfortunate [*miserum*] guilty in proportion to its freedom, and enslaved in proportion to its guilt, and therefore enslaved in proportion to its freedom. Unhappy man [*miser*] that I am, who will deliver me from the shame of this bondage (Rm 7:24)? Unhappy I may be, but I am free. I am free because I am a man, unhappy because I am a slave. I am free because I am like God, unhappy because I am in opposition to God.[73]

Bernard's treatise *Grace and Free Choice* begins and ends with God's mercy, upon which our salvation depends.[74] In between, he goes into detail about the wretchedness of our fallen human condition. The freedom from *miseria*, given us in Adam, was lost by original sin;[75] our native freedom is captive to [actual] sin.[76] This freedom will be restored to us in heaven;[77] meanwhile, everything in this present life involves *miseria*, and nothing is more miserable than false joy.[78]

Saint Ælred elaborates on this false joy:

> The blind perversity of miserable man is lamentable enough. Although he desires happiness ardently, not only does he not do those things by which he may obtain his desire but rather, with contrary disaffection [*proniori affectu*], takes steps to add to his misery. In my opinion, he would never do this, if a false

---

72. Ded 5.3; Luddy 2:419.
73. SC 81.9; CF 40:165-6.
74. Gra 1; CF 19:54; Gra 42; CF 19: 100,107; Gra 48; CF 19:107.
75. Gra 7; CF 19:62.
76. Gra 10; CF 19:66.
77. Gra 12; CF 19:67.
78. Gra 14; CF 19:70.

image of happiness were not deceiving him, or a semblance
of real misery frightening him off from happiness.[79]

Yet it is precisely the experience of one's own *miseria*—self-
knowledge, coming to oneself as did the prodigal son—that opens
one to receive the divine mercy. When the soul recognizes its
wretchedness, Bernard explains, "it starts in astonishment and
says: 'Is it possible for such wretchedness to make a man happy?'
Whoever you are, if you are in this frame of mind, do not despair;
it is mercy, not misery, that makes a man happy, but mercy's natural
home is misery."[80] Again he tells his monks: "The first step for the
wretched man extricating himself from the depths of vice is the
mercy which makes him merciful to the son of his mother (Is 49:15),
to be merciful to his soul, and thereby pleasing to God (Si 30:24—a
favorite scriptural verse). In this way he emulates the great work
of divine mercy."[81] This mercy toward oneself must precede mercy
toward others, for "Just as pure truth is seen only by the pure of
heart, so also a brother's miseries are truly experienced only by
one who has misery in his own heart. You will never have real
mercy for the failings of another until you know and realize that
you have the same failings in your soul."[82] But it also leads to it:
"People who admit that to make satisfaction [for their sins] is
beyond them . . . fly from justice to mercy, by the road Truth
shows them: 'Blessed are the merciful for they shall obtain mercy'
(Mt 5:7)."[83] As Isaac of Stella sees it, "Only mercy obtains mercy."[84]
"God so desires mercy," Baldwin affirms, "that he himself testifies
to this (Mt 9:13; Hos 6:6), and there is almost nothing he desires as
much, almost nothing he would rather have than mercy. . . . [A
sacrifice of mercy] obtains mercy from the God of mercy."[85]

79. Spec car 1.22.63; CF 17:123.
80. Conv 12; CF 25:46.
81. QH 11.9; CF 25:209; Conv 29; CF 25:65; John of Forde, S 50.8; CF 44:53.
82. Hum 6; CF 13:35.
83. Hum 18; CF 13:46; Guerric, S 32.5; CF 32:78.
84. S 3.11; CF 11:24.
85. S 7.19, 21; CSQ 29:3, 251-2.

* * *

The great work of God's mercy was the redemption, beginning with the Son's coming to us as man. This was a mystery particularly dear to Bernard: "Our Creator, seeking what was lost . . . came down in mercy to where [our first parents] lay in misery. . . . It was not his intention to remain with them in misery, but to raise them from it by his mercy,"[86] and to Guerric: "He compassionately took misery upon himself so that from his misery he might show compassion to the miserable."[87] Guerric elaborates:

> The eternal birth [of Christ] is certainly more full of glory, but the temporal more lavish in mercy, in that it is on my behalf who needed mercy. I was besieged by misery, misery I could not expiate. Show your mercy to us (Ps 84:8) who are not yet fit to see your glory. . . Show us, Lord, your mercy, cloaked in our misery and working the cure of the miserable by a new kind of mercy drawn from our very misery. For this, the art of mercy, has blended God's beatitude and man's misery in making them one in the Mediator.[88]

"Christ," says Baldwin, "is himself our mercy, he 'in whom we have all the grace of life and truth, all hope of life and strength'" (Sir 24:25).[89] And as Guerric contemplates the mystery of the Presentation of the child Jesus in the temple, he addresses Simeon: "Embrace God's Wisdom, then, O blessed old man; and may your heart beat high and glow again as it did in youth. Hold God's Mercy tight to your breast, and your grey hairs shall be blessed with mercy" (Ps 91:11).[90]

God's mercy reaches its fullness in the mystery of Christ's passion and death, when, as Guerric explains: "He mercifully

---

86. Hum 12; CF 13:40.
87. S 31.1; CF 32:66.
88. S 6.1; CF 8:37-38.
89. Sac alt 1; SCh 93:88.
90. S 15.3; CF 8:102.

took misery upon himself so that from his misery he might show mercy to the miserable."[91] Bernard, reflecting that "someone else's miseries are truly experienced only by one who has misery in his own heart," sees that Christ has set us an example: "He willed to suffer [*patior*] so that he might know compassion; to learn mercy he shared our misery. It is written: 'He learned obedience from the things he suffered' (Hb 5:8); and he learned mercy in the same way. I do not mean that he did not know how to be merciful before; his mercy is from eternity to eternity (Ps 102:17); but what in his divine nature he knows from all eternity he learned by experience in time."[92] "The Cross," Baldwin asserts, "is the end of misery"[93] for on the Cross "the mercy of God has been plainly placed before our eyes."[94] John of Forde marvels: "'As the heavens are high above the earth' (Is 55:9), so your mercy was even toward those who crucified you,"[95] and Bernard triumphantly exclaims: "Whatever is lacking in my own resources I appropriate for myself from the heart of the Lord, which overflows with mercy."[96] William desires to enter into this open heart of Christ, "the sure seat of your mercy."[97] Elsewhere he speaks of Christ's feet,[98] arms,[99] and face[100] of mercy.

Bernard sees that mercy and judgment are not in opposition: they are the two feet of Christ.[101] Our response to the foot of mercy is hope; to that of judgment, fear, since lingering too long on the thought of judgment leads to despair, and on that of mercy leads

91. Palm 3.1; CF 32: 66.
92. Hum 6; CF 13:35.
93. S 8.8; CSQ 29:3, 278.
94. S 8.6; CSQ 29:3, 277.
95. S 95.3; CF 46:151.
96. SC 61:4; CF 31:144.
97. Med 6.11; CF 3:131.
98. Med 5.9; CF 3:123.
99. Med 9.7; CF 3:148.
100. Med 8.1; CF 3:139.
101. SC 6:5; CF1:35.

to negligence.[102] "Where is true justice, if not from Christ's mercy?
. . . only those are just who have had their sins pardoned through
[Christ's] mercy. . . . his mercy is the well-spring of justice."[103]
Wondering about the relationship of God's justice with his mercy,
John of Forde realizes "the incomprehensible depths of your
mercy. I see, I clearly see, that your charity is your justice, since
indeed you are all charity, our God, you are all justice. With you
to abound with the riches of mercy is absolutely just, because
proper, natural and instinctive."[104] "You are truly just and merciful, O Lord," he exclaims. "Your right hand is filled with justice
(Ps 47:10), and your mercy is full of discernment."[105] Guerric
urges his monks: "Fly from the Judge to the Redeemer, from the
tribunal to the Cross, from the Just One to the Merciful."[106]

* * *

The Cistercians, like other medieval authors, see the psalm
verse "Mercy and truth have met each other" (Ps 84:11) as fulfilled
in the Incarnation.[107] Bernard's first Sermon for the Annunciation
contains an extended parable, really a drama, relating how this
took place, with Mercy, Truth, Justice, and Peace personified.[108]
Another verse the Cistercians are fond of quoting is "All the ways
of the Lord are mercy and truth" (Ps 24:9). Bernard comments: "To
each and every one alike he comes in his mercy and truth. When
we presume upon his mercy and forget his truth, straightaway God
is absent. . . . Nor does anyone hold truth who fails to recognize
present mercy; nor can there be real mercy without truth."[109]
"Happy the soul," muses John of Forde, "in whom mercy and truth

102. SC 6:8; CF 4:36.
103. SC 22:11; CF 7:24.
104. S 10.7; CF 29:199-200.
105. S 13.9; CF 29:246.
106. S 32.5; CF 32:78.
107. SC 6.7; John of Forde, S 13.9; CF 29:245.
108. Ann 1.6-14; Luddy 3:138-152.
109. QH 11.7; CF 25:206-7.

so run to meet each other that it is not as if they merely greeted each other on their journey. No, they clasp hands and embrace, and twined together pace out the whole journey."[110] Nevertheless, they have different functions: "Because mercy is in the merciful God who pities those who 'do not know' (Lk 23:34), it is typical of it to seize on the ungrateful, to draw the unwilling . . . Moreover, it is typical of truth, since it proclaims God's justice and foretells his judgment, to admit them to the taste of the fear of God, as if from the breast of truth."[111] Guerric sums it up: God "grants grace through his mercy, conferring glory through his truth."[112]

* * *

As the Cistercians see Jesus as the personification of divine mercy, it is not surprising that they also call his Mother the "Mother of Mercy." "She is the one-only Mother of Mercy All-High," explains Guerric, "so that in a wonderful way she is fruitful with the fruitfulness of the divine mercy."[113] They rightly give her this title since, as Bernard explains, "She it is through whom 'we have received your mercy, O God'" (Ps 47:10).[114] Guerric addresses her: "O Full of Grace (Lk 1:28), I congratulate and praise you. You gave birth to the Mercy I received,"[115] and John implores her: "Turn those merciful eyes of yours to us."[116] John describes those eyes:

> The virgin mother's eyes are compassion and mercy [*miseratio et propitiatio*]. They are compassion, in that she compassionates sinners; they are mercy, in that she implores

110. S 98.6; CF 46:193; S 13.9; CF 29:246.
111. S 72.5; CF 45:123-4.
112. S 3.3; CF 8.11. S 3:3; CF 8:11.
113. S 15.3; CF 8:102; John of Forde, S 16.32-34; CF 41:18; S 75.8; CF 45:165; Bernard, Dom in oct asspt 15; Luddy 3:260.
114. Asspt 2.2; Luddy 3:225.
115. S 15:3; CF 8:102.
116. S 75.10; CF 45:167. (Both this phrase and the title Mother of mercy, of course, are found in the *Salve Regina*.)

repentance and forgiveness for them. Their pity is infinite, because she keeps people back from sin by following the example of her Son. Their mercy, too, is very rich, because she supports sinners and listens to their prayers.[117]

Bernard lovingly and trustfully invokes Mary as a merciful Mother whose mercy, like God's own, finds its home in our misery:

> O most blessed virgin, let him refuse to extol your mercy who—if there be any—remembers having invoked your assistance and finding you wanting in his hour of need. . . . We praise your virginity, we admire your humility, but because we are so miserable, more consoling to us than either is your mercy; we love your mercy more tenderly, we recall it more frequently, we invoke it more often. And the reason is, because it is to your mercy that we owe the restoration of the whole world and the salvation of all.[118]

Thus it is no wonder that he describes Mary's Song (Luke 1:46-55) as "beginning and ending in mercy." After commenting on the verse "Holy is his name," he quotes the next one, "And his mercy is from generation to generation" and exclaims: "Behold his name! What is it? His mercy."[119]

* * *

If Mary is the Mother of Mercy, surely the Father of Jesus must be the Father of mercy, as already Paul calls him in his Second Letter to the Corinthians (1:3).[120] John sees that "The fatherly love of God draws us to the Father of mercy in hope of pardon and to implore his grace."[121] Bernard explains:

---

117. S 75.5; CF 45:160-1; Bernard, Dom in oct asspt 2; Luddy 3:260.
118. Asspt 4.8; Luddy 3:255.
119. Sent 3.127; CF 55:457, 450.
120. Bernard, SC 73.5; CF 40:79; John, S 103.6; CF 47:37; S 104.3; CF 47:43.
121. S 93.4; CF 46:126; S 13.3; CF 29:235.

It is natural for [the Father] to show mercy, for he finds in his own divine nature the motive and impulse to this. . . . He is called, not the Father of judgments, or of vengeance, but the Father of mercies; not only because mercy appears to belong more to a father than indignation, and because "as a father has compassion on his sons, so has the Lord compassion on those who fear him" (Ps 102:13); but also and especially because he finds in himself the motive and impulse to show mercy, whereas when he exercises judgment or vengeance, the cause is in us.[122]

No wonder Bernard can cry out: "O Father of mercy! O Father of the miserable!"[123] He is the One of whom we read:

"The mercy of God is from eternity" (Ps 102:17). Surely there can be nothing co-eternal with the Father save the Son and the Holy Spirit. And each of these two is not so much merciful, as mercy itself. But the Father himself is also mercy. And these three are not three mercies, but one mercy.[124]

But John sees that each of the three divine Persons has a particular kind of mercy:

It is truly the work of God's fatherly tenderness to implant the disposition to mercy in the human heart; it falls to the Son, God's power and Word, to bring it into action by word and deed; but it was reserved for the Holy Spirit, the font of love, to expand that mercy, strengthen and preserve it.[125]

Towards the end of his life Merton wrote: "One who lives by the mercy of God alone shall have nothing else to live by, only that mercy."[126] Bernard would surely agree, adding that such a one *needs* nothing else. For as he exclaims:

122. Nat 5.3; Luddy 1:413.
123. Ded 5.8; Luddy 2:426.
124. Nat 5.2; Luddy 1:412.
125. S 98.6; CF 46:194.
126. *Seasons*, 181.

Whatever is lacking in my own resources I appropriate for myself from the heart of the Lord, which overflows with mercy. . . . The secret of his heart is laid open through the clefts of his body; that mighty mystery of loving is laid open, laid open too the tender mercies of our God (Lk 1:78). . . . No one shows greater mercy than he who lays down his life for those who are judged and condemned. . . . My merit therefore is the mercy of the Lord. Surely I am not devoid of merit as long as he is not of mercy. And if the Lord abounds in mercy (1 S 24:14), I too must abound in merits. . . . And if the mercies of the Lord are from eternity to eternity (Ps 102:17), I for my part will chant the mercies of the Lord forever (Ps 88:1).[127]

127. SC 61.4-5; CF 31:144.

Chapter 6

LOVING-KINDNESS

Devotio and *Pietas*

The whole life of the Nigerian Cistercian monk Blessed Cyprian Tansi, could be summed up in the title of his biography, *Entirely for God*. This of course is the ideal of every committed Christian; even more of monastics. It is the fulfillment of the first great commandment: "You shall love the Lord your God with all your heart, with all your soul, with all your mind, and with all your strength" (Deut 6:4; Mark 12:30). Christian tradition captures something of this basic disposition in the word *devotio*.

Associated with it, and to some extent synonymous, is *pietas*. Their English equivalents, "devotion" and "piety"—even more, the corresponding adjectives "devoted" and "pious"—have, like many other words derived from Latin, lost much of their original force and become weak and insipid. Looking into their origins and development may enable us to recapture some of their original scope and rich resonances.

* * *

The roots of *devotio* go back to classical Latin.[1] In the course of its history the word underwent a considerable change of meaning. Originally it was associated with the idea of nemesis or fate. A certain balance of good and evil obtained in the world; if it were disturbed, it had to be restored. For that purpose, something or someone had to be destroyed. An animal or person was delivered

---

1. This section owes much to the article "Devotion" in DSp 3:702-14.

over to divine wrath, dedicated to destruction, brought under a curse. In this way the gods would be propitiated and the desired favor obtained from them. Persons could also offer themselves in this way. Saint Augustine refers to the semi-legendary Decii who devoted themselves to death, consecrating themselves by a fixed form of ritual words, ensuring that when they fell and placated the wrath of the gods with their blood, the Roman army should be freed from danger.[2]

Something similar occurs in the biblical accounts of Abraham's sacrifice of Isaac (Gen 22) and Jephtha's daughter (Judg 11:29-40). What was put under the ban in a holy war falls into the same category. The Pharisees who plotted to kill Paul delivered themselves up to destruction by their vow (Acts 23—*devotio* is used in the Vulgate).

In the course of time, *devotio* came to signify the act by which a person or object was dedicated, consecrated, not for destruction but for service, either to a person such as the Roman emperor, or to the divinity. The Nazarite vow (Num 6) was such a consecration; so was the Israelites' offerings for the tabernacle (Exod 35:22). From the external act, it was a logical step to the internal dispositions that prompted the act. This occurred in classical usage, where *devotio* took on the connotations of fidelity, loyalty, and respect, and was applied not only to a citizen but, for example, also to one's father or to a conscientious slave. In the Bible, too, we read of the *mente devota* with which the first fruits were given (Exod 35:30) or the holocausts offered when Ezechia purified the temple (2 Chr 29:31).

If the pagan Romans could show devotion to their gods, how much more fitting it was for Christians toward the true God. So it is not surprising that *devotio* very soon became part of the

---

2. Civ Dei 5.18; FC 8:283. Augustine applies this concept of devotion to Paul's death: S 299.3; *Sermons* 3/8:230, and even to the death of Jesus: S 210.3; *Sermons* 3/6:119. There is an echo of it in Baldwin of Forde's *De sacramenti altaris*: to take the chalice, as Jesus did at the Last Supper, was to consecrate himself [*devotio*] to death: De sacr 2.1; SCh 93:150.

Christian vocabulary. At this stage, it had the meaning Michael Casey ascribes to it: "a religious service characterized by objectivity, sobriety, gravity and even a little stateliness."[3]

Lactantius in *The Divine Institutes* sees it as in some sense the Christian religion itself. Adam was placed in the garden of paradise so that, "being free from all labors, he might devote himself entirely [*summa devotione*] to the service of God his Father."[4] To us, who no longer have access to paradise, "our Father and Lord . . . sent a Guide, who might open to us the way of righteousness; we should therefore "follow him, hear him, obey him with the greatest devotedness."[5]

If *devotio* means wholehearted service of God, one of its clearest manifestations is the celebration of the liturgy. So it is not surprising that we find *devotio* occurring in liturgical texts as an expression of either the worshipers' present dispositions or their aspirations. Typical are these Lenten prayers: "May our devotion [*devotionis affectus*] be made fruitful";[6] "May we who are disciplined by fasting rejoice with holy devotion."[7] *Devotio* and *fides*—the latter word both in the sense of faith and that of fidelity—quite naturally go together; this is particularly evident in Saint Ambrose.[8]

Saint Benedict uses *devotio* twice in the *Rule*, with different connotations. In the first instance, it has overtones of a monk's responsibilities and duties with respect to the Divine Office;[9] monks who say less than the full Psalter with the customary canticles each week "betray extreme indolence and lack of devotion in their service" (RB 18:24). Two chapters later, *devotio* is

3. *Athirst for God*, CS 77:111.

4. Div inst 2.13; ANF 7:62.

5. Div inst 7.27; ANF 7:222.

6. Collect for the fourth Saturday of Lent in the Roman Missal. See also that of the fifth Wednesday of Lent.

7. Collect of the fourth Wednesday of Lent. See also the collect for the fifth Saturday of Lent, and the secret prayer of Passion Sunday.

8. For example, Isaac 4.21, 6.54, 7.57; FC 65:24, 44, 47; Jacob 1.6:23, 2:7:30; FC 65:134, 164; Joseph 1:1:1; FC 65:189.

9. See Adalbert de Vogüé, SCh 182:534, note 24.

linked with the significant word *puritas*, implying genuine, wholehearted, unalloyed; the dispositions necessary for petitioning the Lord God of all things are above all *humilitas* and *puritatis devotio* (RB 20:2).

Saint Leo the Great exhorts his hearers to apply themselves to devotion [*studeatis esse devoti*] by works of mercy.[10] Saint Augustine calls almsgiving and fasting "the two wings of devotion, by which our prayer the more easily ascends to God."[11] The sinful woman of Luke 7:36f. showed her devotion in action, without uttering words.[12]

* * *

For Saint Bernard, devotion begins with what he calls carnal devotion; that is, devotion to the humanity of Christ. Though not its highest form, this is already a great gift of the Spirit. "It seizes the whole heart, and draws it completely from the love of all flesh and every sensual pleasure."[13] By it "one is nourished and strengthened by [its] sweetness to good and honest and worthy actions."[14] Such devotion to Christ is altogether fitting: "Good Jesus, the chalice you drank, the price of our redemption . . . wins our devotion so sweetly, justly demands it, firmly binds it, deeply affects it."[15] But such devotion, however important for the early stages of the spiritual life, must later on be transcended; Christ, risen from the dead, must leave the disciples before they can receive the Holy Spirit[16] and a more spiritual kind of devotion.

For *devotio* is a grace, and a monk has need of it to temper the austerities of his life.[17] God first promises many things which

10. S 21; SCh 49:30.
11. S 206.2; *Sermons* 6:107.
12. S 99.1; *Sermons* 4:50.
13. SC 20.7; CF 4:153.
14. SC 20.8; CF 4:154.
15. SC 20.2; CF 4:148.
16. Pasc 4.2; SBOp 5:111.
17. 1 Nat:7; Luddy 1:388.

he is disposed to give us so as to arouse our devotion by his promises and to urge us to procure by devout prayer what he is ready freely to give us.[18]

Yet before one is ready to receive the grace of devotion, purification is necessary.[19] *Devotio* is the third of the Savior's four fountains; it is preceded by the fountain of mercy in which our sins are washed away, and that of wisdom which slakes our thirst.[20] The water of purification shall be changed into wine when fear is cast out by perfect love (1 John 4:18) and then all the vessels shall be filled up to the brim (John 2:7) with spiritual fervor and joyous devotion.[21]

Using another schema, that of eight days, Bernard calls the seventh day the day of devotion. It is preceded by those of justice, prudence, fortitude, temperance, patience, and humility; being the seventh day, it is "the sabbath of the soul," when we "may live without labor in the midst of all labor;" it enables us to "run on the path of God's commandments, our hearts overflowing with the inexpressible delight of love" (RB Prol. 49).[22]

If, in these examples, *devotio* seems to come at the end, in other places it is viewed as the second of three stages of spiritual development. Just as the Magi offered gold, frankincense, and myrrh to the infant Christ (Matt 2:11), Guerric of Igny tells his monks, so they too can present three gifts. The second of these, coming between the myrrh of penance and the gold of wisdom, is "the sacrifice of praise together with the incense of *devotio*," offered as they devoutly fulfill the Work of God.[23]

In a similar way, Bernard sees *devotio* as the second of the Bride's three ointments. The first of these, contrition,

18. 4 Miss 11; CF 18:57.
19. 2 EpiP 8; Luddy 2:52.
20. 1 Nat 6: Luddy 1:386-7.
21. 2 EpiP 9; Luddy 2:54. Bernard also speaks of the wine of devotion in SC 30.6; CF 7:116.
22. 3 Circ 10; Luddy 1:444.
23. Epi 1.5-7; CF 8:73-4.

is good, made up as it is from the recollection of past sins and poured on the Lord's feet. . . . But better by far is the ointment of devotion, distilled from the memory of God's beneficence, and worthy of being poured on Christ's head.[24]

In Bernard's view, this ointment is surpassed, as we shall see, not by wisdom but by *pietas*.

Bernard sees the feasts and seasons of the Church's year as meant to enkindle our devotion[25] but also urges his monks to celebrate them devoutly,[26] especially the season of Lent.[27] It is his own devotion to Mary which inspired him to write the *Four Homilies in Praise of the Virgin Mother*.[28]

"Prove your devotion," says Guerric, "in love and deed."[29] On the other hand, according to Ælred, "good works make prayer stronger, increase devotion, stimulate love."[30] Devotion can be lost,[31] and Isaac speaks wryly of those "whose devotion depends on how well things go."[32]

Devotion needs the assistance of what is variously called truth, knowledge, enlightenment, or discretion. Bernard speaks of the twofold gift, "the light of knowledge and the fervor of devotion."[33] "Without the restraining power of truth," he says, "devotion can be capricious and uncontrolled and even arrogant."[34] For Gilbert, on the other hand, "Barren in that understanding which is not paired with a contemporary and kindred [*coaeva et germana*] devotion."[35] Baldwin of Forde sees that there can be

24. SC 12.10; CF 4:88.
25. For example, Inno 1; Luddy 1:417; 3 Quad 1: Luddy 2:84-5.
26. For example, 1 Ded 1; Luddy 2:385; AndV 4; Luddy 3:38.
27. 3 Quad 1; Luddy 2:84-5; 4 Quad 1; Luddy 2:98; 6 Quad 4; Luddy 2:110.
28. 1 Miss 13; CF 18:13; 4 Miss 58: CF 18:58.
29. Nat 2.1; CF 8:43.
30. Inst 31; CF 2:84.
31. Guerric, Res 2.5; CF 32:90.
32. S 18.11; CF 11:152.
33. SC 8.6; CF 4:49. See also SC 49.4; CF 31:21; 1 Nov 4.2; Luddy 2:362.
34. SC 74.8; CF 40:93.
35. S 24.2; CF 20:298.

neither devotion without discernment nor discernment without devotion. When the two are joined, "there abounds in us charity with knowledge and knowledge with charity."[36]

It is interesting to see what adjectives our authors use to nuance the meaning of *devotio*. It is to be joyful,[37] personal and peerless,[38] prompt[39] and intense;[40] indeed, it is to be total.[41] John of Forde has a particular fondness for adding descriptive adjectives; among others, he uses spontaneous,[42] overflowing,[43] ecstatic, and tender.[44] Devotion and humility go together; William of Saint-Thierry, in fact, declares that there is no devotion without humility,[45] and for John of Forde, "when the mind is aware of its own weakness, that very fact . . . enriches it with a sort of devout humility."[46]

* * *

Devotio and *pietas* are to some extent synonymous, but there are also differences between them. One of these is illustrated by the fact that the expression *pia devotio* occurs frequently.[47] The adjective mitigates any too stiff or formal implications of the noun. For *pietas* has a broader meaning than *devotio*; whereas the latter word implies a certain formality and stateliness, *pietas*

36. S 3.61-5; Tract 11; CF 41:114-5.
37. Guerric, Pur 3:6; CF 8:119.
38. Gilbert, S 35.3; CF 26:429.
39. Guerric Nat 2.3; CF 8:46.
40. Bernard SC 70.4; CF 7:135.
41. Bernard, SC 70.4; CF 40:40; SC 78.6; CF 40:134; Baldwin S 13.30; Tractate 7; CF 38:198; John of Forde. S 55, Int; CF 44:107; S 100.4; CF 46:218.
42. S 67.4; CF 45:65.
43. S 88.1; CF 46:61.
44. S 68.2; CF 45:77-8.
45. Exp 95; CF 6:75.
46. S108.6; CF 47:97. Compare S 59.8; CF 44:178 and S 70.9; CF 45:105.
47. For example, Augustine, De beata vita 2.11; PL 32:965; Bernard, SC 54.1; CF 31:69; William, Exp 16; CF 6:13; Baldwin S 4.10; Tr 1; CF 38:15; John of Forde, S 76.11, 98.12; CF 45:183, 46:200.

evokes a familial spirit. In its classical usage it can be said to encompass one's duty in all relationships: respect and affection for one's parents and children, solicitude for one's comrades, loyalty to the fatherland, devotion to the gods. It is a virtue highly esteemed by the Romans, and Aeneas, the hero of Virgil's *Aeneid*— who in some way epitomizes the Roman character—displays this quality in all its fullness. At the very beginning of the poem he is characterized as a man remarkable for *pietas*,[48] and the word runs through the poem like a refrain.[49]

Precisely because in Roman thought the objects of *pietas*— gods, fatherland, ancestors—were all of a piece, so to speak, the early Christians' refusal to honor the gods was considered not only impious but also a crime against the state and the whole structure of society. In Christian usage, therefore, the word had to undergo a change in its objects. But despite its political resonances, *pietas* offered the Christian a means for explaining himself to contemporary society.[50] It became an important link between philosophers, and pagans in general, and the missionary Church. It is thus that it is used in the Pastoral and Petrine Epistles, the only places in the New Testament where the word occurs.[51]

Pietas has a broader scope than *devotio*; while the latter is proper only to humans, *pietas* is also a divine quality. There is also both our *pietas* toward God, and our *pietas* toward one another. Although it is sometimes difficult to distinguish these three usages, as far as possible I will try to treat them separately, beginning with divine *pietas*.

If *pietas* was a quality even of pagan gods,[52] how much more so of the God of Christians. The early Fathers, among them Saints Leo the Great and Gregory the Great, speak of the wonderful

48. 1:10.

49. For example, 1.253, 305, 378; 6.9, 688.

50. As its Greek equivalent, *eusebia*, had done for the Hellenistic Jew. See the interesting *Excursus* on *eusebia* and *pietas* in *The Letter to Titus*, trans. and comm. Jerome D. Quinn (New York: Doubleday, 1990), 282–91.

51. 1 Tim 2:2,10; 3:16; 4; 6:5; 2 Tim 3:5; 2 Pet 1:6,7; 3:11.

52. Virgil, *Aeneid* 2.536; 5.688; 12.839.

sacramentum or *dispensatio pietatis*[53] of divine Providence, so wonderful that it makes even the temptations of the evil one turn to our good.[54] A number of the collects of the Roman Missal invoke the *pietas* of God; for example:

> Almighty, everlasting God, the abundance of your *pietas* exceeds all that we desire or deserve; pour out upon us your mercy, forgiving those things of which our conscience is afraid, and bestowing more than we dare ask.[55]

It is especially the Son, whose dwelling place, Bernard says, "is at the source of all kindliness [*fons pietatis*]"[56] who reveals to us the divine *pietas* through the mysteries of his Incarnation and Passion.[57] Ælred sees that in Christ "kindness and power came to meet one another [*pietas et potestas obviaverunt sibi*]."[58] The breast of Jesus, upon which John leaned at the Last Supper (John 13:25), is "the abode [*domicilium*] of *pietas*."[59] For Gilbert, Jesus' breast is "the place of true repose, the calm of understanding, the sanctuary of *pietas*."[60] "O surely," he cries out, "Christ himself is the deep mystery of *pietas*."[61]

Saint Gertrude has a particularly keen sense of God's *pietas*. The very title of her book, *Legatus divinae pietatis* makes this clear, and her biographer states that "God chose her . . . to make

53. Leo, S 3.4; SCh 22:104; Gregory, Mo 2.11.19; SCh 32:284; Di 2.21.4; FC 39:89.

54. Mo 2.43.68; SCh 32:354.

55. SC 42.10; CF 7:218; Div 25.8; SBOp 6/1:193; Ælred, Or 5; CF 2:110-11, and the sequence *Dies irae*.

56. Among many other examples, Leo, S 39; SCh 74:40; Gregory, Mo 11.17, 13.27; SCh 212:66, 284; Bernard, Div 29.3; SBOp 6/1:212; Sent 3.319; CF 55:396-7; Guerric, Nat 1.4; CF 8:41.

57. Inst 31; CF 2:84; an allusion to Ps 84:11: *misericordia et veritas obviaverunt sibi*.

58. Inst 31; CF 2:87.

59. S 12.3; CF 14:152.

60. S 20.10; CF 14:108.

61. Collect for eleventh Sunday after Pentecost. See also, among others, the prayer over the people for the fourth Friday and fifth Wednesday of Lent.

known through her the mysteries of his *pietas.*"[62] "*O Pietas, Pietas*" she calls him;[63] and her prayer, "may your *pietas* compel you to triumph over our evil by pardoning us," runs like a refrain throughout her seventh *Exercise.*[64]

Not surprisingly, the Cistercians dwell also on the *pietas* of the Mother of God.[65] John of Forde urges his monks to "knock at the very gate of *pietas,* the best mother of all, the mother of Jesus."[66] And we cannot forget the tradition that it was the Cistercians who added the invocation *O clemens, O pia, O dulcis virgo Maria* to the *Salve Regina.*

Such *pietas* on God's part invites a return in kind. It is *pietas,* Cassian says, "the piety that belongs to good sons" that makes the soul "address God most familiarly as its own Father" in the Lord's prayer. This same piety impels us "to seek not our own glory but our Father's."[67]

In Augustine's thought, *pietas* is above all "the worship of God."[68] "I find it written in the book of Job: 'Behold, piety is wisdom.'[69] By piety in this passage he means the worship of God. What else is this if not the love of him, by which we now desire to see him and believe that we shall one day see him."[70] This love must be given "freely and for nothing (that, after all, is what piety is)."[71]

The Christian tradition sees *pietas* as one of the seven gifts of the Holy Spirit. These have their source in Isaiah 11:2, and as

62. Herald 1.2.2; CF 35:42.

63. Exercise 7, CF 49:137.

64. CF 49:122-46. Compare Bernard, SC 11.2; CF 4:70.

65. For example, Bernard, Assp 4.9; Luddy 3:256; Hum 53: CF 13:23; Guerric, Assp 1.3; CF 32:169.

66. S 111.10; CF 47:141.

67. Conl 9.18; Ramsey 340-1.

68. Among other places, Civ Dei 1.3; FC 14:118.

69. This is neither the Septuagint not the Vulgate reading of Job 28:28. It is not known from what version Augustine took it. Perhaps he was misquoting from memory.

70. De Trin 12.14; FC 45:36.

71. S 56.4; *Sermons* 3:97.

happens in a number of other cases, depend on the Vulgate's choice of translation. The Hebrew text, in listing the spirits or qualities that will fill the Messiah, gives "fear of the Lord" twice. This quite probably happened by accident, through dittography. But the Septuagint uses two different words, *eusebeia* and *phobos*, followed by the Vulgate's *pietas* and *timor Domini*; hence the seven gifts.

Augustine begins a long tradition of linking these gifts with the seven Beatitudes of Matthew 5:4-9; they are seven stages in the ascent to God. The last mentioned by Isaiah, fear of the Lord, corresponds to the first Beatitude: that of the poor in spirit. After that, "*pietas* coincides with the meek, for if a person piously searches the Sacred Scripture and does not reprehend what as yet he does not understand, he honors the Sacred Scripture and consequently does not resist it. This is meekness."[72] "It is necessary to have our hearts subdued by *pietas*, and not to run in the face of Holy Scripture, whether when understood it strikes at some of our sins or, when not understood, we feel as if we could be wiser and give better commands ourselves."[73]

Gregory the Great interprets the seven sons of Job as the seven gifts of the Spirit. That of *pietas* "fills the innermost heart with works of mercy;"[74] it is given to us to counteract our hardness of heart.[75] It enables us to have compassion on others in their tribulations.[76]

Bernard sees the gift of *pietas* as given to combat the vice of *curiositas*; it recalls the soul to herself, "draws her back into her inner heart."[77] Indeed, "it completely refashions the soul [so that] recalled to her origin, to that worship of God which, in her wicked

72. Serm in monte, 1.4.11; FC 11:27. See also S 347.3; *Sermons* 10:89.
73. De doctrina Christiana 2.7.9-11; NPF 2:537.
74. Mo 1.35.48; SCh 32:234.
75. Mo 2:49.77; SCh 32:37.
76. Hiez 2.7.7; Gray 235.
77. Div 14.2; SBOp 6A:135; Sent 3.4, 98; CF 55:190,324. Compare Augustine, S 265.4; *Sermons* 7:238: "Let curiosity take her departure, *pietas* take her place."

curiosity and imprudence, she had abandoned, she cries out 'it is good for me to adhere to God.' (Ps 72:28)"[78]

William puts it slightly differently. "The spirit of fear," with which the soul's reformation begins, "will develop into the spirit of *pietas*, where it begins to taste new grace, and begins to love and reverence God."[79]

William also takes up the quotation from Job used by Augustine.[80] He gives the following description of *pietas*: "it is the continual remembrance of God, an unceasing effort of the mind to know him, an unwearied concern of the affections to love him."[81] For William, *pietas* is an *affectus*,[82] a sense,[83] but above all the state of soul attained "when God's grace . . . has restored [our] nature."[84]

Divine *pietas* toward us inclines us to show the same quality toward one another. Saint Ambrose's view of *pietas* is that of one formed in the classical tradition. Its object can be one's parents,[85] brothers,[86] children.[87] Indeed,

> Piety [toward others] . . . is the most basic of all virtues, both as regards human affairs and heavenly discipline. Piety is a friend of God, gratitude towards parents. It wins the Lord over, it is a bond of friendship, an honoring of God, the recompense of parents and the tribute of sons. Piety, I say, is the tribunal of the just, the portion of the needy, a shelter for the poor, and leniency towards sinners.[88]

78. Sent 3.89; CF 55:286.
79. Nat am 5; CF 30:57.
80. For example, Ep 26, 278; CF 12:18; Nat am 7: CF 30:57.
81. Ep 27; CF 12:18.
82. Exp 19; CF 6:14.
83. Exp 74, 203; CF 6:62, 163.
84. Exp 172; CF 6:139.
85. Exp in Lk 8:73; SCh 52:132.
86. Joseph 1:12:69; FC 65:230.
87. De bono mortis 8.36; FC 65:96. See also Ep 83.10; FC 26:491.
88. Exp in Ps 118.45; PL 15:1468.

In *The City of God,* Augustine explains how the different meanings of *pietas* flow from one another:

> In its strict sense, [it] ordinarily means the worship of God. However, it is also used to express a dutiful respect for parents. Moreover, in everyday speech, *pietas* means mercy or pity. This has come about, I think, because God commands us especially to practice mercy, declaring that it pleases him as much or more than sacrifices.[89]

Saint Benedict sees especially the paternal side of *pietas.* At the very beginning of his *Rule* he speaks of "the advice of your loving father [*pii patris*]" (RB Prol. 2); the same loving Lord "who assures us, 'I do not wish the death of the sinner, but that he turn back to me and live'"(Ezek 33:11; RB Prol. 38). It is this father who "in his *pietas* shows us the way of life" (RB Prol. 20). The abbot in his turn must be "devoted and tender as only a father can be [*pium patris ostendat affectum*]" (RB 2:24) and "imitate the loving [*pium*] example of the Good Shepherd" (RB 27:8).

The Cistercians insist that *pietas* express itself in works.[90] However, "no degree of *pietas*," Bernard warns, "may be preferred to that suggested by the Wise Man: 'Have pity on your own soul, pleasing God.'"[91] *Pietas* consists in distrust of ourselves and perfect trust in God.[92] Ingratitude dries up the source of *pietas*;[93] no wonder then that William links *pietas* and *gratias.*[94]

Bernard's most eloquent description of *pietas* is as the third ointment. As we have seen, the first two ointments are those of compunction and devotion. Good as these are,

89. Civ Dei 10.1; FC 14:118.

90. Bernard, SC 3.4, 18.5,6, 37.2; CF 4:19, 137, 7: ; Par 7; CF 55:93; Div 33.5; SBOp 6A:225; Guerric, Pur 4.4; CF 8:123; Gilbert, S 35.5; CF 26:431.

91. SC 18.3; CF 4:135. Compare Qui hab 3.1; CF 25:129.

92. Div 54; SBOp 6A:279; Sent 3.120; CF 55:408.

93. SC 51.6; CF 31:45.

94. Rom Pref, 2; CF 27:16, 71.

there is another, far excelling these two, to which I give the
name *pietas*, because the elements that go to its making are
the needs of the poor, the anxieties of the oppressed, the
worries of those who are sad, the sins of wrong-doers, and
finally, the manifold misfortunes of people of all classes who
endure affliction even if they are our enemies. These elements may seem rather depressing, but the ointment made
from them is more fragrant than all other spices (Sg 4:10),
for it bears the power to heal.

It is used to anoint not merely the feet of Jesus (Luke 7:37f.) or
his head (Mark 14:3f.) but the whole Body of Christ—that is, the
Church, or perhaps even the whole of humanity.[95]

Bernard's friend, Guigo I, prior of the Grande Chartreuse, puts
it succinctly: "How does Truth [*Veritas*] treat you? With *pietas*. Thus,
then, should you treat others."[96]

---

95. SC 10.4-12:10; CF 4:63-86. See also Sent 1.9, 2.169; CF 55:120,176; Div 87.6,
88.1; SBOp 6a:333-4. It is interesting to compare this with Bernard's schema in his
early work *The Steps of Humility*. There the sequence is contrition, compassion,
and contemplation: from self to others and finally to God. The later sequence of
self, God and others may be simply a case of *diversa non adversa*, but it may also
indicate a development in his thought.

96. Med 95; CS 155:83.

Chapter 7

CONSENSUS

Consentire

What does it mean to consent? To agree to something or someone; to accept something done or proposed; ultimately, to commit oneself. Nowhere is the fearsome privilege and responsibility of consent more evident than at the moment of the annunciation to Mary. Saint Bernard imagines all humanity breathlessly waiting for her reply to the angel, telling her: "The price of our salvation is being offered you. If you consent, we shall immediately be set free."[1] A modern poet expands the scene:

> The engendering Spirit
> did not enter her without consent.
> God waited.
>
> She was free
> to accept or to refuse, choice
> integral to humanness.
>
>   . . .
>
> This was the minute no one speaks of,
> when she could still refuse.
>
> A breath unbreathed,
>   Spirit,
>   suspended,
> waiting.

1. Miss 4.8; CF 18:53.

She did not cry, "I cannot, I am not worthy,"
Nor, "I have not the strength."
She did not submit with gritted teeth,
                    Raging, coerced.
Bravest of all humans,
                    Consent illumined her.
The room filled with its light,
the lily glowed in it,
                    and the iridescent wings.
Consent,
                    courage unparalleled,
opened her utterly.[2]

So the crucial issue is with what, or whom, the consent or agreement is made. In the last analysis, there are only two possibilities: either we consent to God and all that implies—his law, his will—or we consent to sin. Hence the battle within us which Saint Paul so graphically describes in Romans 7:16: "I consent to the Law, that it is good, but I find a different law in my members.'"

Although Paul speaks of the struggle between his flesh *carne* and his mind *mens*, Origen sees the possibility of their agreement: "When the flesh does not oppose the spirit but obeys it and agrees with it, it is good."[3] In fact, "by their union, flesh and spirit, like a married couple, increase and multiply, generating good feelings and useful thoughts."[4] Cassian, perhaps influenced by Origen, envisions a time when "the flesh has stopped lusting against the spirit and has given its consent to [the latter's] desires and to virtue. They begin to be mutually joined to one another by a most stable peace."[5]

2. From "Annunciation," by Denise Levertov, from *A Door in the Hive* (New Directions, 1989), quoted in John Shea, *Starlight* (New York: Crossroad, 1992), 124–26.

3. Hom in Ex 13.5; FC 71:384.

4..Hom in Gen 1.15; FC 71:68.

5. Conl 12.11.1; Ramsey 448.

Saint Augustine, however, who knew from experience the strong pull of "the other law," spoke more often of the struggle. He warned his people that although they could not entirely avoid feelings of concupiscence or covetousness—he also spoke of delight or pleasure—they must not consent to them: "What is the meaning of 'it is not I performing that thing'? It means, I covet [*concupiscio*] in the flesh, I don't consent [*consentio*] in the mind. . . . There you have the battle." Quoting 1 Corinthians 15:55: "Where, death, is your challenge [*contentio*]?" he explains: "If the challenge of death is our struggle, it is now not I doing it, but sin that lives in me. (Rm 7.17) It's the covetousness of the flesh that he calls sin; I covet, but don't consent with the mind, and covetousness does not cease to incite me to evil. That's the challenge of death."[6] "In my mind I serve the law of God by not consenting [*non conscendiendo*] but in the flesh the law of sin by feeling lust [*concupiscendo*]."[7]

"Don't consent and [covetousness] doesn't conceive. What's the meaning of 'entering into temptation'? (Mt 26.41) Consenting to a bad desire. You've consented [*consensisti*]? You've entered [*intrasti*]. At least be quick to come out."[8] "Sin is in you when you feel the pleasure *delectaris*, but it reigns only if you consent [*consenseris*]."[9]

Therefore, his advice is: "When [the devil] begins to suggest evil acts to you, get rid of him before pleasure surges up and consent follows."[10] For "Satan cannot coerce an unwilling victim; it is within your power to consent or not to consent."[11] We must even go so far as to "cut it off and throw it away from you" (Matt 18:8-9); that is: "Don't consent. . . . In our bodies, our various parts form a unity by consent, they live by consent, they

6. S 77A.2; *Sermons* III/3.328.

7. S 151.8; *Sermons* III/5.45.

8. S 77A.3; *Sermons* III/3.329.

9. En in Ps 50:3; *Psalms* III/16:412.

10. En in Ps 48, 1.6; *Psalms* III/16:357.

11. En Ps 91:3; *Psalms* III/17:347. Cf En Ps 57:19; III/17:127.

are connected with each other by consent [*consensione*]. Wherever there is dissent [*dissensio*], it means a disease or a wound."[12]

The source of our struggles goes back to the very beginning of human history, when "[Adam] consented with his wife, already beguiled by the serpent, to disregard God's commandments."[13] Subsequently: "From the face of the earth he was cast forth by pride who, after agreeing to taste the forbidden fruit in order to be like God, hid himself from the face of God"[14] (Gen 3:8). Unlike that of the devil, it was "the temptation from without which seduced [Adam] and became his sin when he gave his consent to it."[15]

Augustine does, however, also use "consent" in a good sense; he speaks of "praising [God] not only with the tongue, but with tongue and life in agreement."[16] "The pure and upright of heart are united to [God] . . . by their agreement of heart in innocence and rectitude."[17] Explaining what an "upright heart" is, he calls it one that accepts whatever suffering comes his way, as sent by God for his true welfare, and does not complain or rebel. "God does not yield [*consentit*] to your heart; you must yield to the heart of God."[18]

One last example must be quoted in full in Latin, to illustrate Augustine's skill with words. Commenting on verse three of Psalm 149, "Praise his name in chorus," he explains what a chorus is: "*Chorus est consensio cantantium. Si in choro cantamus, concorditer cantemus.* [A chorus is agreement in singing. If we sing in chorus, we sing concordantly]."[19]

As can be seen, consent lends itself to the sort of wordplays the Latin writers delighted in. Saint Gregory the Great makes a double one: "Whoever feels temptation hears the voice [of the

---

12. S 81:4; *Sermons* III/8:362.
13. En Ps 7:7; *Psalms* III/15:67.
14. En Ps 1:4; *Psalms* III/15:69.
15. En in Ps 18,1:14; *Psalms* III/15:201.
16. En in Ps 49:30; *Psalms* III/17:408.
17. En in Ps 24:21; *Psalms* III/15:252.
18. En in Ps 63:18; *Psalms* III/17:262.
19. En in Ps 149.7; *Psalms* III/20:498.

tempter], but only the one who consents listens. [*Qui sentit, audit; qui consentit exaudit*]."[20] He enumerates the stages of temptation and sin: "We become aware of sin by suggestion, we are overcome by pleasure, and by consenting we are also put in bonds."[21] In the *Moralia*, he expands in typically methodical manner:

> We sin in our hearts in four different ways; we sin in our deeds likewise in four different ways. In the heart we sin by the stages of suggestion, delight, consent and bold self-defense. The suggestion comes from the adversary, the delight from the flesh, consent from the spirit and bold self-defense from our pride. . . . So the ancient enemy broke down the rectitude of the first man by these four blows. The serpent persuaded, Eve delighted, Adam consented, and after he was questioned he refused to confess his guilt, boldly defending himself. . . .The serpent persuaded: for the hidden enemy secretly suggests wickedness to the human heart. Eve delighted: for the senses of the flesh at the serpent's bidding soon enslave themselves to delight. Adam, who had been set over the woman, consented: for when the flesh is captured by delight, even the spirit is weakened and turns away from its rectitude. When he was questioned, Adam declined to confess his fault: for the spirit is hardened more wickedly to cling to the audacity of its own ruination just because by sin it is separated from the truth.[22]

* * *

The Cistercians take up some of the themes we have seen in the patristic writings. They distinguish between *sensus* and *consensus*.[23] They attribute the Fall to the consent of Adam[24] and Eve[25]

20. Mor 4.35.69: PL 75:676.
21. Reg pas 3.29.85; ACW 11:202.
22. Mor 4.27.49; PL 75:661.
23. Bernard, SC 49.8; CF 31:28; Div 13.4; SBOp 6,1:133, Baldwin of Forde, S 2.61; Tr 4; CF 38:125.
24. Bernard, Sent 3.69; CF 55:239; Baldwin, S.8:77; Tr 6, CF 38:181.
25. Bernard, Par 7.6; CF 55:94.

to the suggestion of the devil. They enumerate the stages of the downward path; usually three, as Bernard, for example: "Our will was defiled by the enticements of temptation, by the effects of earthly delights, and by the disordered character of our choices [*consensus exordinante.*]"[26] Sometimes the stages are expanded to seven, of which consent is the fourth:

> Sinners are seized first by negligence concerning their own welfare, then by curiosity about things outside themselves which have no relevance to them, and then by lust for those things. Consent follows lust, bad habit follows consent, contempt follows habit, and malice—that is, an attachment to sin and delight in sinning—follows contempt. Negligence retards us, curiosity impedes us, lust binds us, consent ties us harshly down, bad habit drags us further along, contempt forces us headlong, and delight in sin locks us in the prison of despair, because a sinner despairs when he has arrived at the depths of evil.[27]

Conversely, there are seven stages in the return to God, and Saint Bernard links them to the seven gifts of the Holy Spirit: "the Holy Spirit sets fortitude against consent, lest the soul be overcome to the point of giving consent."[28]

In an extended analysis of the "carnal man" (Rom 7:14), Baldwin of Forde stresses the difference between concupiscence and feeling on the one hand, and consent on the other: "It is not always in our power to feel or not to feel the passions of our members, but it is in our power to consent [to them]. For there is no [consent] without our will [*voluntate*]."[29] "What one feels comes from his weakness; the fact that he doesn't consent comes from his strength/virtue. [*Quod sentit, infirmatitis est; quod non consentit, virtutis est*]."[30] Someone who "gives his full consent to

26. Bernard, Sent 3.5; CF 55:192; also Sent 1.25; CF 55:128, Sent 3.2; CF 55:183.
27. Bernard, Sent 3.5; CF 55:192.
28. Sent 3.4; CF 55:191.
29. S 3.33; Tr 11 CF 41:103.
30. S 3.33; Tr 11 CF 41:104.

concupiscence gives life to the 'body of sin,' which then becomes the servant of sin."[31] "But by the law of discipline, [this sinful] consent is restrained, the body of sin is destroyed, and the flesh chastised, and as a result, the mind is not subjected to the flesh according to the law of the flesh, but the flesh serves the mind according to the law of the mind."[32] Thus begins the journey back to God, for "Righteousness begins with our consent to it."[33] Our growth in righteousness follows "an ordered series of stages;" after consenting to it, we become disposed to it, put it into effect, practice it, make it habitual, then reap its fruits [*consensu, affectu, effectu, usu, habitu et fructu*]."[34]

In the eighty-fifth Sermon on the Song of Songs, Bernard describes how we begin to consent to God, with an unexpected exegesis of Matthew 5:25:

> We read in the Gospel how the Word says: "Agree [*esto consentiens*] with your adversary quickly, while you are in the way with him, so that he does not hand you over to the judge, and the judge to the executioner." What better counsel could there be? It is the counsel of the Word, who is himself the adversary of our carnal desires, when he says, "These people always err in their hearts." (Ps 94:10) If you who are listening to me have conceived a wish to flee from the wrath to come (Lk 3:7), you will, I think, be anxious to know how you are to agree with this adversary who seems to threaten you so terribly. This will be impossible unless you disagree [*dissentias*] with yourself and become your own adversary, and fight against yourself without respite in a continual and hard struggle, and renounce your inveterate habits and inborn inclinations. But this is a hard thing. If you attempt it in your own strength, it will be as though you were trying to stop the raging of a torrent, or to make the Jordan run backwards. What can you do then? You must

31. S 3.46; Tr 11 CF 41:108.
32. S 3.48; Tr 11 CF 41:109.
33. S 19.11; Tr 9,4 CF 41:71.
34. S 19.11; Tr 9,4 CF 41:71.

seek the Word, to agree *consentias* with him, by his opera-
tion. Flee to him who is your adversary, that through him
you may no longer be his adversary.[35]

Bernard devotes an entire treatise, *On Grace and Free Choice*,
to the positive aspect of consent, consenting to God. He begins
by distinguishing the respective roles of God and the human
person in achieving the latter's salvation. Salvation is a coopera-
tive project; since "God is the author of salvation and the free
willing faculty merely capable of receiving it; none but God can
give it, nothing but free choice receive it," by giving its consent,
and in this consent, the whole of salvation lies. "What part does
God play? He saves. What part does free choice play? It is saved."
Thus "to consent is to be saved [*consentire salvare est*]."[36]

Unlike sense perception and natural appetites, which we
share with the animals, voluntary consent is "a self-determining
habit of the soul. Its action is neither forced nor extorted . . . If
it is compelled in spite of itself, there is violent, not voluntary
consent. Where the will is absent, so is consent, for only what is
voluntary may be called consent. Hence, where you have consent,
there also is the will."[37] Another way of defining consent is "a
spontaneous inclination of the will."[38] It is precisely this consent,
"voluntary and not necessary, that proves us to be just or unjust,
and also, meritedly, makes us happy or miserable. Such consent,
on account of the imperishable freedom of the will and the inevitable judgment of the reason always and everywhere accom-
panying it, is, I think, well called free choice."[39]

Realistically, Bernard admits that in our present, fallen state,
our power to choose freely has been diminished; we are unable
to completely avoid falling into sin. Still, "in this sinful flesh and
in this evil of the day, it is no small wisdom not to consent to sin,

35. SC 85 1; CF 40:196-7.
36. Gra 2; CF 19.54-5.
37. Gra 2: CF 19:55.
38. Gra 4; CF 19.57; also Ælred, Spec 1.10.10; CF 17:103.
39. Gra 4; CF 19.59.

and this, with Christ's grace, we are able to do."[40] We can even
be so bold as to "presume to apply to ourselves the title of 'God's
fellow workers' (1 Cor 3.9), cooperators with the Holy Spirit,
meriters of the kingdom, in that we have become united with the
divine will by our own voluntary consent."

Summing up, Bernard says:

> Are we to say then that the entire function and the sole merit
> of free choice lies in its consent? Assuredly. Not that this
> consent, in which all merit consists, is its own doing, since
> we are unable even to think anything of ourselves (2 Cor
> 3.5), which is less than to consent. But by bringing about
> the change of our ill will, [God] joins it to himself by its
> consent; and by supplying consent with faculty and ability,
> the operator within makes his appearance outwardly
> through the external work that we perform.[41]

How closely does the union of God and the soul resemble
that of the Father and the Son? Bernard calls the latter *consubstan-
tiale*, a union of substance. Father and Son have only one will,
"and where there is only one will, there can be no agreement or
combining or incorporation or anything of that kind. For there
must be at least two wills for there to be agreement." He concedes,
however, that we can speak of consensus between Father and Son,
"provided that it is understood as not a union [*unionem*] of wills,
but a unity [*unitatem*] of will."[42] The union between God and the
soul, on the other hand—agreement/harmony/*consensio* of will—
he calls *consentibile*. "We think of God and man as dwelling in
each other in a very different way [than Father and Son], because
their wills and their substances are distinct and different; that is,
their substances are not intermingled, yet their wills are in agreement [*consentaneas*]. This union is for them a communion of wills
and an agreement in charity."[43] Nevertheless, it is such a close

40. Gra 26; CF 19.83.
41. Gra 46; CF 19.105; also Isaac S 46:15; SCh 339:128.
42. SC 71.9; CF 40:56.
43. SC 71.10; CF 40:56.

union that it makes them two in one spirit (Gen 2:26), or indeed one spirit (1 Cor 6:17).[44] For Bernard, "To love thus is to be married, because [the Bride] cannot love thus and not be loved, so that in the consent of two is a complete and perfect marriage."[45]

Other Cistercians also speak of the union with God in love that *consensus* brings. "Whoever is truly alive," says Baldwin, "gives his consent to the will of God, since life is in his will (Ps 29:6) . . . for it is by giving our consent to his will that God wants us to love him."[46] Ælred of Rievaulx agrees: "To join one's will to the will of God, so that the human will consents to whatever the divine will prescribes, and so that there is no other reason why it wills this thing or another except that it realizes God wills it: this is surely to love God."[47] So John of Forde prays: "As far as my will is concerned, may it all be turned into your will, so that from now on, my will may not be called my will, but your will should take its place. This means that my soul will be blissfully married to you, her lawful spouse, in other words, reverently and humbly united to you by the full consent of a pure will."[48]

In this life, William of Saint-Thierry sees, the Holy Spirit transmutes all our affections "into the perfect purity of [God's] love, and the truth of [his] purity, into full accord with [his] love."[49] This is already a great grace. However, "When the day breaks and the shadows retire (Sg 2:17), Bridegroom and Bride will no longer be present to each other in agreement [*consentiendum*], but for their mutual enjoyment [*fruendum*].

44. SC 71.7; CF 40:54.
45. SC 83.6; CF 40:302.
46. S 15.45; Tr 15, CF 41:172.
47. Spec 2.18.58; CF 17:200.
48. S 110.10; CF 47:126.
49. De cont 11; CF 3:36.

Chapter 8

SPONTANEITY

Sponte

Although *sponte*, 'spontaneously,'[1] is not a technical term in the Bible or the patristic and monastic tradition, it has enough interesting applications to warrant a study. Rather than following a strictly chronological order, we will consider some of the ways *sponte* is used. To call attention to the word, I will consistently translate it literally, even though "freely" or "of one's own accord" would at times give a smoother English rendition.

Étienne Gilson describes *spontaneous* as "the manifestation of the will in its pure form," "a movement explicable without the intervention of any factor outside this movement itself, a movement which on the contrary contains in itself its own complete justification."[2] Such an action, gesture, gift, may reveal a person's deepest orientation more fully than do more deliberate, reflected ones.[3]

---

1. With its cognates; it is most often used in the adverbial form.

2. *The Mystical Theology of Saint Bernard*, CS 120 (Kalamazoo, MI: Cistercian, 1990), 90 (hereafter, *Mystical Theology*).

3. "It does not, perhaps, in the last analysis, matter all that much what you do with forethought; what really matters, what is really revealing, is what you do without thinking, what you do if you are woken up suddenly in the night, what you do when you do not have time to work out how to respond. It is this that will reveal what kind of person you are, that is what is important" (Simon Tugwell, *The Beatitudes: Soundings in Christian Traditions* [Springfield, IL: Templegate, 1980], 85).

Spontaneity is willingness, but goes beyond it; it may be said to be willingness carried to the nth degree.[4] Its opposites are necessity [*necessitas*], and compulsion [*invitus*]. It is a quality inherent in the power of free choice, which, the tradition affirms, is the quality in human beings that makes them most like God. "If we will," says Saint Augustine, "no one else wills for us, and this movement of the will is spontaneous, for it has been granted to the soul by God."[5] Saint Bernard describes free choice as "something clearly divine which shines forth in the soul like a jewel set in gold";[6] it is by "freedom of choice that [the will] was made in the image of him who created it."[7] What a noble possibility is given us: "That person is better who is good freely and willingly than the one who is good by necessity."[8] Indeed, as Saint Anselm puts it: "When a [rational] being desires what is right, he is honoring God, not because he is bestowing anything upon God, but because he is spontaneously subordinating himself to God's will and governance, maintaining his own proper station in life within the natural universe, and, to the best of his ability, maintaining the beauty of the universe itself."[9] This freedom of choice was not given to us to be used arbitrarily: "Angels and men were given free will not to attain what they wanted, but to will what they ought."[10] This is true spontaneity. Sin, on the other hand, which Saint Ælred of Rievaulx describes as a spontaneous movement away from the Creator and toward the

4. "For Anselm, will, spontaneity and absence of necessity are equivalent terms." Étienne Gilson, *The Spirit of Medieval Philosophy* (Notre Dame, IN: U of Notre Dame P, 1991), 209.

5. De div quaes 8; FC 70:40.

6. SC 81.6; CF 40:162.

7. Gra 6.19; CF 19:75.

8. De div quaes 2; FC 70:27; see Anselm, Cur 1.10; *Anselm of Canterbury, the Major Works* (Oxford UP), 280 (hereafter, *Major Works*): "True obedience is that which occurs when a rational being, not under compulsion *necessitate*, but spontaneously, keeps to a desire which has been received from God."

9. Cur 1.15; *Major Works*, 288.

10. See Augustine, Civ Dei 14.11; FC 14:376-77: "The will's choice is truly free only when it is not a slave to sin and vice."

creature,[11] is a false, perverse kind of spontaneity. For, in Hans Urs von Balthasar's terms, our finite freedom can fulfill itself only in the context of Infinite Freedom; theonomy, not autonomy, is true freedom.[12]

Yet the ability to choose freely includes the possibility of making the wrong choice, and that, in fact, is what revelation tells us the first humans did. Although this fall remains a mystery, the tradition affirms that it was spontaneous: that is, without necessity or compulsion. Speaking for the tradition, Anselm says: "It was through the capacity to sin freely and spontaneously and not of necessity that ours and the angelic nature first sinned."[13] "When the soul falls away from the unchangeable Good," says Augustine, "this falling away is spontaneous; for, if the will had merely remained firm in the love of that higher immutable Good which lighted its mind into knowledge and warmed its will with love, it would not have turned away in search of satisfaction in itself and, by so doing, have lost that light and warmth."[14] And Saint Gregory: "[The human race] when created for life in the freedom of its own will, was spontaneously made the debtor of death."[15] In fact, according to Anselm, "In the Garden, man was created without sin, as if he were placed there as God's deputy, in a position between God and the devil, the intention being that he might overcome the devil by not consenting when the devil recommended sin by means of persuasion. In the event that man were not to sin despite the devil's persuasion, this would vindicate and honor God and confound the devil. . . . And although man was easily capable of doing this, he allowed himself to be conquered by persuasion alone, not under forcible compulsion";[16]

11. Anima 2; CF 22:99.

12. *Theo-Drama II* (San Francisco: Ignatius, 1990), 189–334.

13. Lib arb 2; *Major Works*, 177. (For the sin of the angels: "A spontaneous fall deprived the [fallen] angels of their high station." Gregory, Mor 15.54.61; PL 74:1113; compare Mor 4.5.5; PL 75:642; Augustine Civ Dei 12.9; FC 14:160).

14. Civ Dei 14.1; FC 14:376-77.

15. Mor 17.33.46; PL 76:32.

16. Cur 1.22; *Major Works*, 307.

"the devil did not gain his hold over man by violence, rather, it was man who had gone over to the devil spontaneously."[17] Isaac of Stella also says that Adam "fell spontaneously and foolishly";[18] "Man spontaneously descended from his God-given state of image and likeness."[19]

Baldwin of Forde describes the unhappy plight of the fallen: they "are miserable of their own free will, *sponte*, and the more they think themselves blessed, the more miserable they actually are."[20] Bernard's eighty-first *Sermon on the Song of Songs*, echoing chapter seven of the Letter to the Romans, describes the contradiction inherent in the human condition: "In a strange and evil way, [man is] both held as a slave in voluntary and yet irresistible bondage, and free."[21] Elsewhere he says: "When [the will] inclines spontaneously toward the bad, it makes a person nonetheless free and spontaneous in the bad. He is not forced to be evil."[22]

Since human freedom was not completely destroyed by sin, the possibility of regaining our lost spontaneity remains. But we cannot do it by ourselves; as Anselm remarks: "Man spontaneously brought upon himself a debt which he cannot repay."[23] Bernard agrees: "Although the soul fell of itself, it cannot rise of itself, because the will is weak and powerless . . . it has enslaved itself . . . not only that, but it continues to do so."[24] The initiative has to come from God, and Bernard imagines God saying: "If I compel him against his will he will be only an ass and not a man. In that case, he would not come freely and spontaneously."[25] But God is able to draw a person without using violence, Anselm explains: "Since everyone is 'drawn' or 'impelled' by something

17. Cur 1.7; *Major Works*, 272.
18. S 6.1; CF 11:47.
19. S 55.11; SCh 339:296.
20. S 3.5; Tr 11:CF 41:92.
21. SC 81.9CF 40:165.
22. Gra 4.9; CF 19:65.
23. Cur 1.24; *Major Works*, 310.
24. SC 81.8; CF 40:163.
25. De div 29.2; SBOp 6:1:211.

which he steadfastly desires, it is not inappropriate for it to be asserted of God that he 'draws' or 'impels' when he is the giver of such a desire. In this 'drawing' or 'impulsion' there is no inevitable element of violence which is understood to be present; rather a spontaneous and heartfelt wish to hold on to the good desire which has been received."[26] Augustine, commenting on the verse, "O God, in converting us you will give us life," says: "It is not as though we were converted to you spontaneously, with your mercy playing no part, and then you give us life . . . even the conversion is your gift."[27]

This conversion may be looked upon as beginning a process of regaining our original spontaneity. Saint Benedict, without using the word, sees such spontaneity as the goal of the monastic life and describes it twice in his *Rule*. At the end of the Prologue, in order to encourage the beginner, he says that though the way of returning to God by the labor of obedience may seem narrow, when we have progressed in it, "we shall run with enlarged heart and the unspeakable sweetness of love in the way of the Lord's commandments" (Prol. 48-49). Again at the end of chapter 7 he assures us that after having climbed all the degrees of humility, we will arrive at that perfect love of God by which we do everything "without effort, as though naturally, from habit, out of love for Christ, good habit and delight in virtue" (7.67-69).

Bernard, like Cassian before him,[28] sees the journey to God as proceeding by stages and successive relationships to God: one begins to relate to God through fear, as a slave, then through hope of reward, as a hireling, and finally through love, as a son: "Sometimes even a slave can do God's work, but it is not done spontaneously; he is still base. The hireling can do it also, but not *gratis*; he is seen to be lured on by his own cupidity."[29] But for the son, that is, for the one who loves God, laws "are not imposed

26. Cur 1.10; *Major Works*, 280.
27. En in Ps 84.9; *Psalms* 3/4:210.
28. Conl 11; Ramsey 409-22.
29. Dil 34; CF 13:126.

unwillingly, but given freely"; love makes them "a pleasant yoke and a light burden."[30] Thus Bernard makes explicit the link between love and spontaneity that Benedict has implied; the only thing that can convert souls, that is, make them act in accord with their own nature as originally intended by God, is love.[31] He puts it in one of the brief epigrams of which he is master: love "affects [us] spontaneously, and makes [us] spontaneous [*sponte afficit, et spontaneum facit*]."[32]

Although in his later works Bernard never expressly connects love and spontaneity, one finds an echo of it in the way he speaks of love in his eighty-third Sermon on the Song of Songs: "Love is sufficient for itself. . . . It is its own merit and its own reward. Love needs no cause beyond itself, nor does it demand fruits; it is its own purpose. I love because I love; I love that I may love."[33]

How is this kind of love and spontaneity to be expressed? Even under the Old Covenant, provision is made for spontaneous gifts to God, beyond those prescribed by the Law.[34] But Christians are invited to offer not gifts but themselves in service to God. Bernard, speaking for the monastic tradition, sees profession as a monk as a more radical and complete gift of self. He reminds monastics that they have spontaneously made profession; now they are justly bound to honor the vows they were not bound to make.[35] Indeed, he proposes that instead of keeping within the narrow bounds of what they are obliged to by their vows, they should be eager to respond with spontaneity in the breadth of love, reaching out in boundless liberty.[36] As John of Forde puts

30. Dil 35; CF 13:126.

31. Bernard calls the state in which we are led to the good through the probity of our own will *spontanea honestate*, as natural to us, that is, the recovery of our original uprightness: Sent 3.32; CF 55:219.

32. Dil 17; CF 13:110.

33. SC 83.4; CF 40:184.

34. For example Lev 7:16; 22:18; Num 29:39; Deut 16:10; 1 Chr 29:5, 9.

35. Ep 1.8; 2.6; *Letters* 6, 14; cf Ælred, Spec 3.34.80; CF 17:278.

36. Pre 12; CF 1:114.

it, they should "deny every inclination of their own will through the spontaneous love of obedience."[37] Even if, says Bernard, "during the time of discipline, which will always have some pain in it, [the monk] tries to break the chains to which spontaneously and joyously he submitted, after this temptation he will rejoice to have submitted to them. He will then be able to sing with confidence: 'I will willingly sacrifice to you'" (Ps 53:6).[38]

Such a person is described by Augustine. Commenting on the name *Jonadab* in the title of Psalm 70, which he takes to mean "the Lord's Spontaneous One," Augustine asks: "What does that suggest? It evokes a person who serves God willingly and freely. What would it mean to be the Lord's Spontaneous One? 'The good things I have vowed to give you, and the praise I will render to you, are within me, O God' (Ps 55:12). What is it to be the Lord's Spontaneous One? 'Of my own free will I will offer sacrifice to you' (Ps 53:8). If the apostolic teaching warns a slave to serve his human master willingly and not under compulsion, and by this service to make himself free in his own spirit, how much more must you serve God with your total, undivided free will?"[39]

If love and spontaneity are so inseparable that Gilson can say "charity *is* spontaneity and freedom,"[40] surely God, who *is* love (1 John 4:8), must be spontaneity? Only once does the Vulgate use *sponte* with reference to God, but interestingly enough, in it, spontaneity and love are juxtaposed. At the end of the book of Hosea, YHWH, having expressed his affection for Israel as that of a betrayed husband for his errant wife, or a scorned father for his ungrateful child, sums up the unshakeable constancy and the extravagance of his love in the cry: "I will heal their defects, I will love them *sponte*, for my wrath is turned away from them" (Hos 14:5).

37. S 6.3; CF 29:135-6.
38. Sent 3.32; CF 55:218.
39. En in Ps 70(1).1.2; *Psalms* 3/17:414-5.
40. *Mystical Theology* 96.

The New Testament finds other ways to express the spontaneity of God's love: it is *gratis*, prevenient; it surpasses all understanding. The Christian tradition does not take up the quotation from Hosea, although we do find reference to the spontaneous Incarnation and Passion of the Son: "God, just and justifying," says Saint Gregory the Great, "spontaneously descends to the suffering human race, and frees the prisoners of death by virtue of his justice."[41] Christ "spontaneously willed to succumb to the death to which we come unwillingly [*invite*]."[42] The spontaneity of Christ's death plays an important, even central, role in Anselm's soteriology. It appears early on in his *Cur Deus homo*: "The Father did not compel [Christ] to suffer death, or even allow him to be slain, against his will, but of his own accord he endured death for the salvation of man."[43] Likewise, "the Son did not spare himself, but spontaneously gave himself up for us. . . . By following the will received from the Father invariably and spontaneously, the Son became obedient to him even unto death, and learned obedience from what he suffered."[44] Toward the end of the work Anselm explains that it was precisely because Christ offered his life without necessity or obligation that his death was redemptive: "No one except [Christ] ever gave [or ever could give] God what he was not obliged to lose, or paid a debt he did not owe. But [Christ] spontaneously offered to the Father what there was no need of his losing, and paid for sinners what he owed not for himself."[45] And "without satisfaction, that is without voluntary payment of the debt, God can neither pass by the sin unpunished, nor can the sinner attain that happiness he had before he sinned."[46] In his prayers, too, Anselm speaks of "the wisdom and goodness of him who spontaneously took

41. Mor 13.46; SCh 212:312.
42. Hom xl in ev; CS 123:167.
43. Cur 1.8; *Major Works*, 275.
44. Cur 1.10; *Major Works*, 280.
45. Cur 2.14; *Major Works*, 347; cf Cur 2.11: *Major Works*, 329.
46. Cur 2.19; PL 158:391; *Major Works*, 302.

up the Cross,"[47] who "spontaneously died that the sinner might live."[48]

The Cistercians also speak of the spontaneity of the Incarnation and death of Christ, though more from a devotional than a theological perspective. William of Saint-Thierry contrasts our humility, which consists in self-knowledge and the truth of our human condition, with that of "the God-man, who abased himself spontaneously to the lowest degree of the human condition in order to raise man up."[49] "Preferring other men to himself, Christ willed to die for the wicked that they might live; he spontaneously submitted himself to evil men and was unjustly judged by them."[50]

In his meditation on the Last Supper, Baldwin of Forde speaks of how Christ "broke [the bread] to break the anger of God. . . . By his indestructible force he stood in the breach [*confractione*] (Ps 105:23), not broken [*infracto*]. But he broke himself when spontaneously he offered his flesh to be broken in suffering."[51] Likewise, "to take the chalice was a mystical sign of what was about to happen: it was to dedicate himself to death, to take it upon himself willingly. . . . He took the chalice, because he spontaneously accepted death."[52] "My Lord Christ Jesus," Isaac of Stella exclaims, "does all that he does either led or sent or called or ordered; he does nothing on his own. . . . However, to his passion he hastens spontaneously and willingly."[53]

It is John of Forde, however, who most frequently associates spontaneity and Christ—some sixteen times. Jesus "spontaneously took upon himself the weakness of our fall";[54] "He is truly spontaneous, [because] he did not come to do his own will, but

47. Orat 4.11; *The Prayers and Meditations of Saint Anselm* (Harmondsworth, England: Penguin, 1973), 102.

48. Orat 2.7; *The Prayers and Meditations of Saint Anselm*, 95.

49. Exp 108; CF 6:88.

50. Exp 110; CF 6:89.

51. De sac 2.1; SCh 93:130.

52. De sac 2.1; SCh 93:150.

53. S 30.1; SCh 207:180.

54. Sermo in dom palm 5; CF 47:261.

the will of him who sent him" (John 6:38).[55] John stresses the spontaneity of Jesus' obedience, "how prompt and eager, how joyful and sweet, how patient and constant."[56] "Spontaneously he offered himself to the gibbet to be crucified."[57] "Who, then," John muses, "would not run forward to be wounded, making a spontaneous and devoted offering of his soul to receive the wound of so great a love?"[58] "Freely and spontaneously, and with glad good will, I will accept the cup of salvation from the hand of the Savior."[59]

May Christ Jesus, the Lord's Spontaneous One par excellence, enable us to follow him in the spontaneity of love.

55. SC 65.11; CF 45:48.
56. SC 9.7; CF 29:186; compare SC 10.5; CF 29:195.
57. SC 25.9; CF 39:156; compare SC 56.10; CF 44:134.
58. SC 33.7; CF 43:56.
59. SC 22.8; CF 39:111.

Chapter 9

SENSING GOD

The Spiritual Senses, Especially *Odor* and *Gustus*

Is it possible to describe in human language an experience of the transcendent, ineffable God, to "express the inexpressible despite all the obstacles that lie in the way?"[1] Mystics of all ages have made the attempt. In doing so, they have resorted to images of hearing, touching, seeing—even smelling and tasting the divine. These metaphors taken from the senses whereby we perceive material objects in the world outside us imply analogous faculties within us by which we come to perceive the immaterial, transcendent God with a direct, intuitive knowledge. These faculties came to be called the interior or spiritual senses. Saint Augustine gives a description of them that has never been surpassed:

> What is it that I love when I love You? Not the beauty of any bodily thing, nor the order of seasons, nor the brightness of light that rejoices the eye, not the sweet melodies of all songs, nor the sweet fragrance of flowers and ointments and spices: not manna nor honey, not the limbs that carnal love embraces. None of these things do I love in loving my God. Yet in a sense I do love light and melody and fragrance and food and embrace when I love my God—the light and the voice and the fragrance and the food and embrace in the soul, when that light shines upon my soul which no

---

1. Karl Rahner, "The 'Spiritual Senses' according to Origen" in *Theological Investigations* 16 (New York: Crossroad, 1983), 81. Rahner calls this article, written in 1932, "of decisive importance for his ideas, pointing to a line of thought which remained operative, albeit in a concealed way, in his later work."

place can contain, that voice sounds which no time can take from me, I breathe that fragrance which no wind scatters, I eat the food which is not lessened by eating, and I lie in the embrace which satiety never comes to sunder.[2]

In recent times, not much attention has been paid to the spiritual senses; they are not mentioned in either the *New Catholic Encyclopedia* or the *New Dictionary of Catholic Spirituality*. But the concept retains its interest and value, and deserves to be better known.

Both terms of the expression "spiritual senses" have a wide variety of meanings and resonances, which we cannot go into here. The very expression may seem paradoxical, uniting as it does the two extremes of the human being. Origen in fact emphasizes the paradox and speaks of "a sensuality that has nothing sensual about it."[3] Basing himself on Proverbs 2:5 he teaches that Solomon already knew of two kinds of senses: "the one mortal, corruptible, human; the other immortal, spiritual and divine."[4] Yet the very fact of juxtaposing "spirit" and "senses" implies the unity of body and soul, the exterior and the interior, and their interaction. Hans Urs von Balthasar gives this explanation of how the exterior and interior senses interact: "a fully human act of encounter [with God] necessarily has not only to include the senses, but to emphasize them, for it is only through the senses and in them that man perceives and acquires a sensibility for the reality of the world and of Being." This is all the more so in the Christian revelation where "God appears to man right in the midst of worldly reality. The center of this act of encounter must, therefore, lie where the profane human senses, making possible the act of faith, become 'spiritual,' and where faith becomes 'sensory' in order to be human."[5]

2. Conf 10.27.38, 10.6.8; *Conf* 262, 242.
3. Contra Celsus 1.48; SCh 132:204.
4. Peri arche 1.1.9; ANF 4:245.
5. *The Glory of the Lord*, vol. 1 (San Francisco: Ignatius, 1982), 365. See the whole section, 365–407.

Although we have been referring to them as spiritual senses, it might be more accurate to call them "senses of the heart," "heart" being understood in its biblical sense, as the place where God bears witness to himself.[6] Scripture speaks of the hidden person of the heart (1 Pet 3:4) and the inner self which is renewed day by day (2 Cor 4:16). The goal of the Christian life, according to Saint Paul, is to become a spiritual person (Rom 8:9-11), one who is led by the Spirit (Gal 5:26). Developing the capacity of our spiritual senses is an important part of this process.[7] One whose spiritual senses are fully operative is described by von Balthasar as having recovered "the original and richly abundant capacity to perceive God and divine things."[8]

All the spiritual senses have their source in the Bible, as Origen sees it:

> Scripture says, "the commandment of the Lord is lightsome, enlightening the eyes" (Ps 18:9). Let him then tell us what sort of eyes these are, that are enlightened by the light of the commandment! And again, "he that has ears to hear, let him hear!" (Mt 13:9) What ears are these, whose possessor alone is said to hear the words of Christ? And again: "for we are the good odor of Christ unto God" (2 Co 2:15); and, among other passages: "O taste and see that the Lord is sweet!" (Ps 33:9) And what else does it say? "And our hands have handled of the Word of life." (1 Jn 1:1)[9]

It is by means of these senses that God draws us to himself. Augustine speaks from his own experience:

6. *Theological Dictionary of the New Testament*, vol. 3 (Grand Rapids, MI: Eerdmans, 1965), 611.

7. It is interesting that Pope Paul VI mentions "spiritualization of the senses" as a characteristic of those who have "effectively created unity and openness in the depth and steadfastness of their life in God." *Evangelium Testificatio* (1971), n. 34.

8. *The Glory of the Lord*, vol. 1 (see note 2), 369.

9. *Commentary on the Song of Songs* 1.4; ACW 26:77-8.

> You called and cried to me and broke open my deafness:
> and You sent forth Your beams and shone upon me and
> chased away my blindness: You breathed fragrance upon
> me, and I drew in my breath, and now I pant for You: I
> tasted You, and now hunger and thirst for You: You touched
> me, and I have burned for Your peace.[10]

Even one of these senses, according to Origen, exerts a powerful attraction:

> The Bride, who has associated with herself the many maid-
> ens . . . relates that she is running towards the fragrance of
> the Bridegroom's ointments under the compulsion of one
> single sense, the sense of smell alone. (Sg 1:2) . . . . What,
> do you think, will they do when the Word of God takes
> possession of their hearing, their sight, their touch, and their
> taste as well, and offers excellences from himself that match
> each single sense according to its nature and capacity?[11]

No matter which sense is involved, it is always the same Christ who is at work:

> Perhaps, as the Apostle says, 'for those who have their
> senses exercised to the discerning of good and evil,' (Heb
> 5:14) Christ becomes each of these things in turn, to suit the
> several senses of the soul. He is called the true Light, there-
> fore, so that the soul's eyes may have something to lighten
> them. He is the Word, so that her ears may have something
> to hear. Again, he is the Bread of life, so that the soul's palate
> may have something to taste. And in the same way, he is
> called the spikenard or ointment, that the soul's sense of
> smell may apprehend the fragrance of the Word. For the
> same reason he is said also to be able to be felt and handled,
> and is called the Word made flesh, so that the hand of the
> interior soul may touch concerning the Word of life. But all

10. Conf 10.27.38; *Conf* 262.
11. *Commentary on the Song of Songs* 1.4; ACW 26:77-8.

these things are the One, same Word of God, who adapts himself to the sundry tempers of prayer according to these several guises, and so leaves none of the soul's faculties empty of his grace.[12]

Saint Augustine stresses the interiority of these senses; to find them one must "'Return to your heart' (Is 46:8 LXX). In your body you found eyes in one place, ears in another; do you find this in your heart? Or is it that in your heart you do not have ears? Show me the eyes, ears, nostrils of your heart."[13] They are the means "by which we distinguish what is just from what is unjust."[14] "If you have senses within you, all these senses within you take delight in the delights of justice. If you have eyes within you, use them to look upon the light of justice. . . . Likewise if you have ears within you, listen to justice."[15]

At times, the interior senses seem to be inoperative, as we can tell from this poignant lament of Saint Anselm:

> Still, Lord, you hide from my soul in your light and beauty, and therefore it still lives in darkness and in misery. I look all around, but I do not see your beauty. I listen, but I do not hear your harmony. I smell, but I do not gather your fragrance. I taste, but I do not know your savor. I touch, but I do not feel your yielding. For, Lord God, it is in your own unutterable manner that you have these things; you have given them to what you have created in a manner that can be felt, but the senses of my soul have been hardened, dulled, blocked by the ancient sickness of sin.[16]

12. Ibid., 2:9; ACW 26:162.

13. In Ev Io 18.10; FC 79:135-6. Saint Benedict also uses the expression "ear of the heart": RB Prol. 1.

14. Civ Dei 11.27; FC 14:231.

15. S 159, quoted by Jean Mouroux, *The Christian Experience* (New York: Sheed and Ward, 1954), 275–76.

16. Pros 17; *The Prayers and Meditations of Saint Anselm*, trans. Benedicta Ward (Harmondsworth: Penguin, 1973), 258.

Saint Bernard mentions the spiritual senses in a somewhat different sense, comparing them to five kinds of love.[17] William of Saint-Thierry expounds this idea:

> The soul possesses her own senses. . . . For as the body has its five senses by which it is joined to the soul by the instrumentality of life, so, too, the soul has her five senses by which she is joined to God by the instrumentality of charity. This is why the Apostle says: "Be not conformed to this world but be reformed in the newness of your sense [*in novitate sensus vestri*]."(Rom 12:2)[18]

Besides the five spiritual senses, William speaks of "the sense of love" [*sensus amoris*] which seems to encompass them all: "[The soul] loves and her love is her sense whereby she senses him whom she senses."[19] "The vision of God is brought about by the sense of love by which God is seen."[20]

The constant teaching of the tradition is that the activity of the spiritual senses is in proportion to the discipline of the physical ones. One must free oneself from the domination of the latter, "so that the eye of the soul has clarity of vision to the extent to which we close the eye of the body."[21] William seems to recall this when he describes how Bernard as a novice at Cîteaux mortified his exterior senses, going on to say, "with [Bernard's] interior senses now enlightened by love, he began, often and most enjoyably, to experience the sweetness that breathed down to him from above."[22] Bernard is perhaps remembering this experience when he writes:

> The wisdom that is good and true, as holy Job experienced it, "is drawn out of secret places." (Jb 28:18) Why then seek

---

17. Div 10; SBOp 6a:121-4.
18. Nat am 15-20; CF 30:72-7.
19. Spec fid 94: CF 15:70.
20. SC 94; CF 6:77.
21. Rahner (see note 1), 88.
22. Vita Bern 4.20; trans. Martinus Cawley (Lafayette, OR: Guadalupe Translations, 1990), 28.

it from without, in your bodily senses? Taste resides in the palate, but wisdom in the heart. Do not look for wisdom with your eyes of flesh, because flesh and blood will not reveal it to you, but the Spirit. (Mt 16:17) Do not look for it in what the mouth tastes, for it is not found in the land of those who live for pleasure. (Jb 28:13) Do not look for it in the hand's touch, for a saintly man says: "If my mouth has kissed my hand, that is a great iniquity and a denial of God." (Jb 31:27-8) . . . Though Isaac was wise, his senses led him astray. (Gn 27:23) Only the hearing that catches the Word [*percipit verbum*], possesses the truth.[23]

To entice the clerics of Paris to turn from the delights of the world, Bernard describes the greater delights of a "paradise of inner pleasure":

There the bride's nard breathes forth its utterly fragrant perfume (Sg 1:11) and other aromatic oils flow when the south wind blows and the north wind hies away. (Sg 4:16) In the midst of the garden is the tree of life, (Gen 2:9) the apple tree mentioned in the Song, more precious than all the trees of the woods, whose shadow refreshed the bride and whose fruit was sweet to her taste. (Sg 2:3) There the radiance of continence and the beholding of unblemished truth enlighten the eyes of the heart; (Eph 1:18) and the sweet voice (Sg 2:14) of the inner comforter gives joy and gladness to the hearing as well. (Ps 50:10) There the nostrils inhale the exquisite scent of hope, of a rich field which the Lord has blessed. (Gen 27:29) There eagerly we have a foretaste of the incomparable delights of charity.[24]

For Baldwin of Forde, the soul that "lives and senses [*vivit et sensit*] in God and by him, draws a sort of analogy with the things it knows through the bodily senses."[25] "The interior senses

23. SC 28.8; CF 7:94.
24. Conv 13.25; CF 25:60.
25. Tr 4.44; CF 38:118.

[*sensus mentis*] have their own pleasures and delights."[26] Baldwin relates the five senses to five virtues: the soul "senses God within itself and touches him spiritually by faith, smells him by hope, tastes him by charity, hears him by obedience, and sees him by contemplation."[27] There is reciprocity: not only does the soul touch, taste, hear God, but God also touches, tastes, listens to the soul.[28]

The soul "who wants to know nothing, but only Jesus," says John of Forde, finds that he himself is the land flowing with milk and honey, and walks about it, enjoying her spouse's fragrance, embraces, conversation and beauty.[29] Indeed, the bride "is dearest when she is only concerned with her beloved, with his embraces and kisses, his addresses, his anointings, his fragrance."[30]

The spiritual senses play a large part in the writings of Saint Gertrude the Great. In a hymn of praise to Christ she exclaims: "In you is the charm of all colors, the sweetness of all savors, the fragrance of all odors, the delight of all sounds, the sweetness of all embraces."[31] The Holy Land, the paradise where the spiritual senses are employed, is the divine heart of Jesus.[32] When Gertrude entered into it, "what she sensed, saw, heard, tasted, touched there, she alone knows, and the One who deigned to admit her to such a union."[33] In her fifth *Spiritual Exercise*, she composes a set of beatitudes:

> Blessed the eyes that see you, O God . . .
> Blessed the ears that hear you . . .
> Blessed the nose that breathes you . . .

26. Sac alt 2.3l; SCh 93:240.

27. Tr 4.44; CF 38:118.

28. Tr 4.45-58; CF 38: 118-24.

29. S 33.3; CF 43:52.

30. S 80.7; CF 45:227.

31. *The Herald of God's Lovingkindness* 3:65; SCh 143:264.

32. P. Doyere, "Sainte Gertrude et les sens spirituels," *Revue d'ascetique et de mystique* 36 (1960): 429–48.

33. *Herald* 3.26; SCh 143:126. See also *Herald* 2.8; CF 35:121-3.

Blessed the mouth that tastes, O God, love, the words of
your consolation . . .

Blessed the soul that clings inseparably to you in an embrace
of love and blessed the heart that senses the kiss of your
heart.[34]

Like Baldwin, Gertrude refers to God's "senses." God's eyes
delight in contemplating her graces, his ears by the words she
addresses to him; her hope is a perfume, her desires are sweeter
to his taste than all else, her love is a tender embrace.[35] On Easter
Day she relates the senses of the glorified humanity of Christ to
the five vowels of the Alleluia.[36] In an eschatological perspective,
she suggests that in the state of glory, the unity of our interior
and exterior senses will be restored, and even the latter will receive a sort of spiritual activity.[37]

Each of the spiritual senses merits an extensive treatment.
Here we will explore the two that are perhaps the most intrigu-
ing: the senses of smell and taste.

ODOR: THE SENSE OF SMELL

What is more enticing and at the same time more elusive
than a pleasant odor: the scent of lilacs, the fragrance of new-
mown hay, the aroma of baking bread. So even this, in some ways
the lowliest of the five senses, can be used as an analogue for our
experience of God, the One who attracts and yet eludes us.

Burnt offerings were prominent in Israelite worship. Although in its early history they bore witness to the primitive and,
to us, crude notion that YHWH was pleased by the odor of the
burning sacrifice and could be propitiated by it, under the influence of the prophets, this idea, along with the concept of sacrifice
in general, became spiritualized and interiorized. Gradually, the

34. SCh 127; CF 49: 90-1.
35. *Herald* 3:50:2; SCh 143:220. See also *Herald* 1:3:5; CF 35:47.
36. *Herald* 4:27:4; SCh 255:264.
37. See SCh 143:365.

"sweet odor" became a technical term referring to the dispositions of the offerer: self-giving, devotion, prayer; and it was these
that made the sacrifice acceptable to God. Since Christ's dispositions were utterly perfect, Saint Paul could apply the phrase to
his self-offering and hold it up as a model for Christians: "Walk
in love, as Christ loved us, and gave himself up for us, an oblation and sacrifice to God for an odor of sweetness" (Eph 5:2). He
could also claim that he and his associates were the good odor
of Christ (2 Cor 2:14).

It was above all the Song of Songs, which speaks so often of
scents, perfumes, incense—myrrh, cypress, flowers, spices, spike-
nard and saffron, sweet cane and cinnamon—that became a
source for mystics who wished to describe the experience of
God.

The tradition developed the theme of the spiritual sense of
smell in varied and sometimes unexpected ways. This sense is
described by von Balthasar as "what is popularly called 'having
a nose for,' but in relation to the things of God."[38] So Origen says
that "whoever has a pure sense of smell and through understanding of the divine Word can run after the fragrance of
[Christ's] ointments (Sg 1:4) has a 'nose' that is sensitive to spiritual fragrances."[39] On the other hand, says Gregory the Great, "a
person with a little nose is one who is incapable of discernment,
for by the nose we discern sweet odors from bad. Rightly, then,
the nose symbolises discernment, whereby we elect virtue and
reject sin."[40]

As we have seen, God uses the spiritual senses to attract us,
and this applies particularly to the sense of smell; Origen implies
that it is the first of the spiritual senses to respond to God.[41] Saint
Augustine, for example, after his earliest encounters with God,
retained "a memory of delight and a desire as for something of

38. *Spirit and Fire* (Washington, DC: Catholic UP, 1984), 254.
39. Cant Co schol; PG 17:282.
40. *Pastoral Care* 1.11; ACW 11:41.
41. Com in Cant 1.4; ACW 26:72-8.

which I had caught the fragrance but which I had not yet the strength to eat."[42]

"Truth is a lily," Bernard says, "whose fragrance awakens faith." The magi would not have followed the star had they not been drawn by the secret sweetness of the lily's bloom.[43] This fragrance comes from heaven; Bernard "seems to inhale a three-fold odor of our heavenly country;"[44] he "catches the fragrance of what [he] cannot hear."[45] William calls it "the perfume of eternity."[46] He stresses its strangeness: it is "a whisp of fragrance of an unfamiliar scent" that comes to us as we pray.[47] "Already, Lord, some of your nameless fragrance [*nescio quis odor tuus*] reaches me; if I could only sense it perfectly, henceforward I should search no more."[48]

It is Christ who is the good odor par excellence, "who as no other both radiates fragrance in his own person and alone is personally perceived in all other [saints], however sweet-scented be their perfume."[49] Bernard calls Christ "the fountain of life . . . that divides into four streams. . . . From these four streams as from priceless perfumes . . . so sweet an odor fills the nostrils of the Church, that she is roused even to the four corners of the earth by its sheer delightfulness . . . drawn as by a sweet scent."[50] Many people, says Origen, have had spices:

> the queen of the South brought spices to Solomon (1g K 10:1-2), and many others possessed them; but no matter what any man had, his treasures could not be compared with the odors of Christ, of which the Bride says: "The odor

42. Conf 7.17; *Conf* 178.
43. SC 70.5; CF 40:40-1.
44. Ded 4.6; Luddy 2:413.
45. SC 67.7; CF 40:11; compare Mar 5: Luddy 3:8: "We enjoy not yet the taste but only the fragrance of [heaven's] delights."
46. Cant 1.47; CF 6:39.
47. Nat am 43; CF 3:104.
48. Med 3.4; CF 3:104.
49. Gilbert of Hoyland, SC 27.4; CF 20:334.
50. Bernard, SC 22.4; CF 7:16-7.

of your perfumes is above all spices" (Sg 1:3). I think myself that Moses had spices too, and Aaron, and each one of the prophets; but if I have once seen Christ and have perceived the sweetness of his perfumes by their smell, forthwith I give my judgment in the words: "The odor of your perfumes is above all spices."[51]

Saint Ælred expands on the perfumes of Christ:

"Your robes are fragrant with myrrh and aloes and cassia." (Ps 44:9) O Christ, O Anointed One, how fragrant are these robes of yours. . . . In himself immortal, he became mortal for our sake: hence myrrh. By the presence of his divinity he fills all things; for our sake he emptied himself and became like water poured out: hence aloes. The angels tremble before him, yet he humbled himself, and in obedience accepted even death, death on a cross: hence cassia. . . . Come, then, brethren, let us savor these ointments in our heart by assiduous meditation. Let us consider how sweet the myrrh of his mortality should be for us: by it he has set us free from all mortality. Again, how sweet his abasement should be for us; it raises us up to heaven. And how sweet his humility, which exalts us.[52]

Isaac's exclamation in Genesis 27:27 is often applied to Christ. No one has done so more beautifully than Guerric of Igny, who weaves together passages from all parts of the Scriptures:

Touching his son and breathing the fragrance of Christ, [Isaac] was filled with the memory of the abundance of that fragrance (Ps 144:7) and exclaimed: "Behold the smell of my son is as the smell of a plentiful field which the Lord has blessed." God the Father smelled that same sweet odor and, well pleased with it, had mercy on the human race when his Son offered himself as an oblation and victim to God in the odor of sweetness. (Eph 5:2) By that same sweet odor

---

51. Origen, Hom in Cant 1; ACW 26:272. See also Peri arch 2.6.6; ANF 4:283.
52. Nat 1.29-31; CCCM 2A:33-4.

we are drawn when by conversion we run toward him; the young maidens too are drawn by it when in their love they run after him. (Sg 1:2) There is a fragrance to be perceived in his wonderful preaching, but this is not the same as the fragrance that comes from his vestments and ointments and is, in a manner of speaking, given off even more abundantly by his body itself. That is none other than the virtue which goes out from him (Lk 6:19) to rouse the lukewarm and infuse in them the fervor of love, so as to make them rejoice to run the way of his commandments. (Ps 118:32)[53]

The good odor of the virtues is a common theme. "Sin has a putrid smell," Origen declares, "while virtue exhales sweet odors."[54] In another place he suggests:

Let us see how someone becomes the good odor of Christ (2 Co 2:14). . . . If there is anyone of you in whom there is now no odor of sin, but an odor of justice, the sweetness of mercy, if anyone, by praying without ceasing (1 Th 5:17) always offers incense to the Lord and says, "Let my prayer be directed as incense in your sight" (Ps 140:2), this man has married Cetura [interpreted as meaning "incense"].[55]

This incense is made, Gregory tells us, "when on the altar of our good works, we give off the odor of numerous virtues."[56] "Spiritual discipline, like some heavenly aromatic spices, steeps [the soul] in the pleasantness of spiritual fragrance."[57] Repentance, though its perfume may seem to be the least valuable, "reaches to the very abodes of the blessed in heaven. . . . More excellent and far more precious" is devotion, but loving-kindness "far excels the other

53. Nat BVM 1.3; CF 32:194-5.

54. Origen, Hom 1 in Cant 2; ACW 26:269. See also Origen, *Dialogue with Heraclides* 18; ACW 54:71-2; Bernard, Hum 2:4; CF 13:32; Isaac of Stella, S 52:10; SCh 339:228.

55. Origen, In Gen 11.2; FC 71:170.

56. Mo 1.54; SCh 32bis:246.

57. Ælred, Spec car 3.34.81; CF 17:279.

two."[58] Humility has its own fragrance,[59] so do virginity,[60] mercy and forgiveness,[61] justice,[62] charity and goodness.[63] "The unseen purity of good living is fragrant," says John of Forde; "seeking to please God, for his sake alone, is a sweet-smelling perfume for the Lord our God."[64] The Cistercians particularly stress the fragrance of prayer.[65] Yet "nothing," affirms Gilbert of Hoyland, "breathes so sweet a fragrance as pure charity from the heart."[66]

All these perfumes have their source in Christ. "If the Bridegroom has touched me," exclaims Origen, "I too become of a good odor, I too am anointed with perfumes; and his perfumes are imparted to me."[67] So William prays: "Pour into me your wholly fragrant spirit that . . . the sweet smell of you, Most Sweet, may permeate me ever more and more."[68] For we are "healed and cleansed by contact with . . . the power and fragrance of [Christ's] healthful perfumes."[69] "Christ is the odor of all sweetness," declares John of Forde, and "when Mary Magdalen poured out her ointment, the whole house was filled with the perfume (Jn 12:3) not because it was poured out by those hands but rather because it was poured out on him and therefore straightway returned the fragrance it had received."[70] Gilbert elaborates on the pouring:

58. Bernard, SC 10.6-7, 12.2; CF 4:64-78.

59. Bernard, SC 42.6; CF 7:217; William of Saint-Thierry, Cant 1.77; CF 6:65.

60. Ælred, Inst incl 14; CF 2:63.

61. Gilbert, S 33.4; CF 26:103.

62. Ambrose, *Isaac, or The Soul* 5:45; FC 65:36.

63. Gilbert, S 32.6-7; CF 20:391-3; John of Forde, SC 24.7; CF 39:143; SC 77.7; CF 45:193.

64. SC 85:5; CF 46:31.

65. William of Saint-Thierry, Nat am 43; CF 30:106; Gilbert, SC 34.6; CF 26:419; John of Forde SC 12.2; CF 29:218; SC 51.6; CF 44:64. See also Ambrose, *Isaac* 5.44; FC 65:35.

66. SC 32.6; CF 20:392. Compare John of Forde, SC 77.7; CF 45:193.

67. Origen, Hom 1 in Cant 2; ACW 26:269.

68. William of Saint-Thierry, Med 8.5; CF 3:142.

69. Cant 1.30; CF 6:25.

70. SC 20.3; CF 39:83.

The soul pleases the Beloved and breathes forth a sweeter fragrance, when it has been wholly poured into him, when clinging to him it is fragrant with the ointment of union, with that ointment which overflows from the Bridegroom to the bride. . . . In our Canticle, "when the king is on his couch," (Sg 1:11) then the bride's nard wafts its fragrance, a good fragrance surpassing all perfumes, the fragrance of the Bridegroom, or rather the fragrance which *is* the Bridegroom. For he is the ointment of his beloved, he is her fragrance, for he takes pleasure for his own sake in his beloved, he diffuses his fragrance through her."[71]

Christ's perfume extends to others, and first of all, to his mother. "It is the beauty of [Mary's humility] that the king has desired (Ps 44:12)," says Bernard, "and it is by the sweetness of its fragrance that he has been drawn down to earth. . . . Through the odor and beauty of humility, Mary has found grace with God (Lk 1:30)."[72] Guerric speaks of the myrrh of Mary's chastity and the incense of her devotion.[73] The Church, too, shares this fragrance. "Holy Church ascends as a pillar of smoke of aromatical spices, of myrrh and frankincense and of all the powders of the perfumer (Sg 3:6)."[74] She is perpetually fragrant[75]—fragrant with the love of Christ.[76]

GUSTUS: THE SENSE OF TASTE[77]

How many rich and varied meanings are attached to the word "taste": a flavor, a slight experience, a suggestion or touch,

71. SC 32.8; CF 20:393-4.
72. Asspt 4.7; Luddy 3:254-5. See also Ælred, Ann 1.
73. Ann 1:6; CF 32:38.
74. Gregory, Mo 1:54; SCh 32bis:248; Hiez 2:10:22, Gray 286.
75. Bernard, SC 12:11; CF 4:86; also 67:21; CF 40:8.
76. John of Forde, SC 113:12; CF 47:165; SC 59:8; CF 44:178.
77. Another word for taste is *sapor*; this however would require a separate study because of its relationship to *sapientia*, wisdom. Bernard, for example, writes: "Perhaps *sapientia* is derived from *sapor* because, when it is added to virtue, like some seasoning, it adds taste to something which by itself is tasteless and bitter. I think it would be permissible to define wisdom as a taste [*saporem*] for good." SC 85:8; CF 40:204.

the ability to appreciate what is excellent, a preference or partiality, an inclination. Of all the senses, taste is the most interior. Sight and hearing maintain a certain distance between the object perceived and the subject; touch keeps a certain exteriority. Taste, on the contrary, produces a sort of symbiosis between object and subject; the word "taste" itself designates both the sense which perceives and the quality of the object which is perceived. There is an evident relationship between taste and love, which also tends if not to absorption, at least to compenetration, fusion, reciprocal immersion.[78]

When all this is transferred to the realm of the divine, it is no wonder that saints and mystics through the ages have seized upon the metaphor of taste to express something of the personal, interior, incommunicable experience of God, and have echoed the invitation of the psalmist: "Taste and see how *suavis*, how delightful, delicious, satisfying is the Lord (Ps 33:9)." The first taste of God may, in fact, mark a decisive turning point in the journey toward God. A reality which up to then had seemed distant, exterior, abstract, impersonal, becomes concrete, interior, supremely desirable. Hence Saint Gregory counsels, "You will not get to know the Lord's goodness unless you taste it. Touch the food of life with the tastebuds of your heart, so that trying it may make you capable of loving its sweetness."[79] And Saint Bernard: "Let [someone who desires to be satisfied (Matt 5:6)] endeavor, however little, to experience the taste of righteousness that he may desire it more."[80] It is this experience which effects the transition from interested, self-seeking love of God to loving him for his own sake: "Tasting God's sweetness entices us to pure love more than the urgency of our own needs."[81]

The elect, says Gregory, "are not content to hear words of wisdom, they taste them that they might relish them in their

---

78. "Gout spirituel," DSp 6:626-35.
79. Eu 36:2; CS 123:313.
80. Conv 27; CF 25:63.
81. Dil 26; CF 13:118; OS 1:11; Luddy 3:344.

hearts. . . .What they have heard receives from love a savor which penetrates them to the marrow [*medullitus sapit*]."[82] William of Saint-Thierry resorts to paradox; it is "a taste of sweetness that cannot be tasted."[83]

At the beginning of creation, says Ælred, man's love "was a tasting of God in the interior of his heart."[84] For love, adds William, "is the heart's palate which tastes that you [God] are sweet, the heart's eye which sees that you are good. And it is the place capable [of receiving] you, great as you are."[85] Baldwin of Forde agrees: "It is through love as if through taste, that [the soul] perceives and is perceived [*sentit et sentitur*]."[86]

The senses of smell and taste are related:

> There is something that is excellent alike in taste and smell, something, that is to say, which delights the palate with its sweetness and at the same time pleases the nostrils with its fragrance; it is the apple, and it is the apple's nature to possess both these properties in itself. The Bride, wishing to praise not only the fragrance of the Word, but also his sweetness, says: "as the apple among the trees of the wood, so is my nephew amid the sons"(Sg 2:3).[87]

"'The righteous shall rejoice in the Lord' (Ps 63:11), tasting and knowing what I only perceive by its fragrance," Bernard laments. "He whom the righteous sees face to face, the sinner awaits, and the waiting is fragrance."[88] Simeon, "because he waited in hope (Luke 2:25-35) already knew the fragrance of Christ . . . through the fragrance of expectation he came to the taste of

82. Mo 11:9; SCh 93:132.

83. Nat am 43; CF 30:106.

84. *Sermon on the Nativity*; *Sermones Inediti*, ed. C. H. Talbot (Rome: Apud Curiam Generalem SOC, 1952), 38.

85. Spec car 1:1:2; CF 17:88.

86. Tr 4:55; CF 38:123.

87. Origen, Hom in Cant 2.6; ACW 26:292-3. See also Com in Cant 3;5; ACW 26:180.

88. Bernard, SC 67:6; CF 40:9.

contemplation."[89] "How long," Bernard wonders, "shall we smell and not taste, gazing toward the fatherland and not taking possession of it?"[90]

> The flavor of the vintage does not inebriate before the sweetness of the fragrance has drawn, nor does the joy of full vision fill the soul with gladness if loving reverence for [God's] renown has not allured it first, because unless we have believed we will not understand (Is 7:9) nor will we taste that the Lord is sweet (Ps 33:9). It is faith that smells, experiential knowledge that tastes and enjoys.[91]

The taste of God's presence is varied;[92] even a bitter taste is not to be rejected: "Myrrh . . . has a very bitter taste, but its effect, apart from other useful qualities, is to withstand corruption. What more bitter to the taste, what more wholesome in its effect than the sorrow which moves a sinner to repentance?"[93] "Whoever suffers martyrdom . . . take confidently, as from a Father's hand, the cup which your Father has given you as a fatherly gift. Drink it confidently. If the taste is bitter, the effect is wholly life-giving."[94] "This fear which love purifies does not make away with joy but guards it; does not destroy it but aids its growth; does not make it bitter but gives it a wholesome flavor."[95]

Christ indeed "adapts and fits himself to all requirements."[96] "The Word of God is said to be flesh and bread and milk and vegetable (Jn 6:51; 1 Pt 2:2; Rm 14:1; Hb 5:14) and is named in different ways for the capacity of those believing or the ability of those appropriating it."[97] Christ is the Tree of Life, containing

89. SC 67:6; CF 40:9-10.
90. SC 50:8; CF 31:37. See also Mar 5; Luddy 3:8.
91. Guerric Nat BVM 1:4; CF 32:195.
92. Bernard, SC 31:7; CF 7:129.
93. Guerric, Epi 1:3; CF 8:170.
94. John of Forde, SC 4:7; CF 29:121.
95. Guerric, Pent 1:2; CF 32:112.
96. Origen, Com in Cant 1:4:12; ACW 26:78.
97. Origen, Hom in Exod 7:8; FC 71:312.

every kind of sweetness and spiced with various flavors: his obedience, patience, humility and charity.[98] He is both "the fruit-bearing tree (Sg 2:3) and the mustard tree (Mt 13:32), since he refreshes us with life and pricks us with health, sweet to taste and pleasantly pungent."[99]

There is general agreement that "once one has tasted the good Word and his flesh, and the bread that comes down from heaven, one's palate will suffer no other taste. Because he tastes so sweet and so delightful, all other flavors will seem harsh and bitter."[100] "The sweetness of God so manifests itself to the taste of one who tastes it, that everything relating to the flesh, the world or any other created being becomes insipid."[101] "To savor that sweetness increases our appetite, and we hunger more and more."[102]

But it is also possible to fall away after having tasted the heavenly gift (Heb 6:4).[103] So we hear the lament: "I have tasted wisdom so often, yet I find myself still so insipid. . . . I seem to have come away from the sweetness of the heavenly manna with nothing but a mouth more bitter than before."[104] The true bride-soul, however, continually hungers for what she has once tasted.[105]

The soul that tastes God is nourished by his love,[106] his truth;[107] by the taste of purity, humility, charity;[108] by the delights of

98. John of Forde, SC 119:6; CF 47:236.

99. John of Forde, SC 102:2; CF 47:16-7.

100. Origen, Com in Cant 1:4:13; ACW 26:78.

101. William of Saint-Thierry, Cant 80; CF 6:66. See also Gregory, Hiez 1:10:43; Gray 127.

102. Baldwin of Forde, Sac alt 2:1; SCh 93:132. See also Bernard, Miss 3:6; CF 18:37 and Gertrude, *Exercise* 5; CF 49:74.

103. Guerric, Pent 1:4; CF 32:113-4.

104. John of Forde, SC 24;6; CF 39:41.

105. Bernard, SC 74:3; CF 40:87.

106. Baldwin of Forde, Tr 4:55; CF 38:123.

107. Gilbert, SC 27:6; CF 20:337.

108. Bernard, Quad 5:6; Luddy 2:98.

devotion;[109] by the inner meaning of Scripture;[110] ultimately, by God's wisdom.[111]

But exactly what is it, to taste God? It is something elusive, ineffable; but we catch a glimpse of what it is from William's description:

> Sometimes, Lord, when I, as if with eyes closed, gasp for you, you do put something in the mouth of my heart, but you do not permit me to know just what it is. A savor I perceive, so sweet, so gracious and so comforting that, if it were fulfilled in me, I should seek nothing more. But when I receive this thing, neither by bodily sight nor by spiritual sense nor by understanding of the mind do you allow me to discern what it is. When I receive it, then I want to keep it, and think about it, and assess its flavor; but forthwith it has gone."[112]

It is, as Gregory the Great affirms, a foretaste of heaven.[113]

109. Bernard, Ded 3:2; Luddy 2:402.

110. Bernard, 4 p P 2; CF 53:115.

111. John of Forde, SC 110:12; CF 47:128; see also Bernard, SC 85:8-9; CF 40:204-5; Guerric, Epi 3:6-7; CF 8:890.

112. Contem 12; CF 3:61.

113. Di 2:35:1; FC 39:104. See also Mo 15:47:53; SCh 221:92; 16:19:24; SCh 221:174.

Chapter 10

THE SWEETNESS OF THE LORD

Dulcis and *Suavis*

In its basic meaning, *dulcis* refers directly to the sense of taste, to what is sweet as opposed to what is bitter. This sense quite naturally broadens out to describe all that is pleasant, agreeable, delightful, attractive and desirable. Closely associated with *dulcis* is *suavis*, which has a broader meaning, and can be applied to any one of the five senses. In practice, however, the two words are nearly synonymous. Classical Latin used *dulcis* and *suavis* metaphorically, applying them to songs, to poems, to life itself, and to human relationships of friendship and love.[1] In present-day English, the adjective "sweet" has been overworked and has, so to speak, lost its flavor, but Italians still speak of *la dolce vita*.

* * *

The Hebrew and Greek versions of the Old Testament use "sweet" in the concrete sense, to describe water (Exod 15:25), honey (Judg 14:14; Ezek 3:3, etc.), fruit (Judg 9:11), and also, particularly in the sapiential books, metaphorically: for sleep (Eccl 5:11), light (Eccl 11:7), the words of the wise man (Prov 16:21). The sweetness of honey must have been particularly appreciated by the Hebrews; the promised land was a place where milk and honey flowed (Exod 3:8, 17, and passim); and the excellence of the Torah was evoked by describing it as more desirable than gold and sweeter than honey (Ps 18:11; 118:103). Of special significance

---

1. *Dulcedo Dei*, DSp 3:1777-92.

is the late book of Wisdom, which refers to the manna as "the food of angels, bread from heaven prepared without labor, having in it all that is delicious, and the sweetness of every taste [*omnis saporis suavitatem*]. For your sustenance showed your sweetness [*dulcedinem tuam*], to your children, and serving every man's will, it was turned to what every man liked" (Wis 16:20-21).

It was especially the translation of words for good—*tob, kalos, chrestos*—by *dulcis* and *suavis* in the early Latin versions of the Psalter, retained in the Vulgate, that became the means through which these words entered the Christian vocabulary.[2] Perhaps the translators felt that *bonus* was too general and abstract a term and wanted to add a nuance that would bring out more clearly the special quality of God's goodness. At any rate, henceforth *dulcedo* and *suavitas* would be divine attributes.

The early Christian writers use *dulcis* in a variety of ways, often in contrast to bitterness, in comparing the Old and New Testaments under various aspects. Saint Ambrose, commenting on Exodus 15:23-25, sees both the cross of the Lord[3] and grace[4] as the means by which the bitter water of Mara was sweetened. Origen[5] contrasts the bitterness of the Law, as literally interpreted, with the sweetness of the spiritual interpretation brought by Christ, himself the Tree of life. Later in the same homily, Origen compares the sweetness of the manna to that of the Word of God.

Besides these more objective and dogmatic interpretations, the Fathers gave another interpretation that put the accent more on the interior sweetness of the experience of knowing God. This is exemplified by Origen: "One's palate will suffer no other taste when it has tasted the good Word of God, and his flesh, and the bread that comes down from heaven. Because he tastes so sweet and so delightful, all other flavors will seem harsh and bitter."[6]

---

2. *Dulcis*: Ps 20:4, 24:8, 67:11; Sg 2:3, 2:14, 4:3. *Suavis*: Ps 33:9, 85:5, 99:5, 108:21, 134:9, 144:7, 9; Sg 5:16; 6:3.

3. De mysteriis 3.14; FC 44:10; De sacramentis 2.2.12; FC 44:283.

4. De mysteriis 9.51; FC 44:24; De sacramentis 2.4.12; FC 44:283.

5. Hom in Ex 7.1-3; FC 71:300.

6. In Cant 1.4; ACW 26:78.

One must, however, know how to appreciate this sweetness. Saint Augustine quotes Psalm 30:6: "O how great is the multitude of your sweetness, O Lord;" he replies to someone who questions where this sweetness is: "How am I to show you this treasure of sweetness when the fever of sin has made you lose your sense of taste? . . .Your heart does not possess the sense of taste necessary to relish these good things: what can I do for you?"[7]

Yet there is something that can be done; Saint Gregory the Great explains it:

> Spiritual pleasures increase our inner longing even while they satisfy, because the more we savor them, the more do we perceive that there is something to be loved more. But when we do not possess them, we cannot love them, because their savor is unknown. Who can love what he does not know? The psalmist counsels us, 'taste and see that the Lord is good,' meaning 'you will not get to know his goodness unless you taste it. Touch the food of life with the taste buds of your heart, so that trying it may make you capable of loving its sweetness.'[8]

Saint Benedict, wishing to encourage his young disciples in the Prologue to his *Rule*, abandons his usual sober and restrained language to exclaim, "What, dear brothers, is more delightful [*dulcius*] than this voice of the Lord inviting us? See how the Lord in his love shows us the way of life" (RB Prol. 19-20).[9] And if the monastic life might seem strict and narrow at the beginning, he assures them that "as we progress in this way of life and in faith, we shall run on the path of God's commandments, our hearts overflowing with the inexpressible delight of love [*inenarrabili dilectionis dulcedine*]" (RB Prol. 49).

---

7. En in Ps 30.6; *Psalms* III/15, 351-2.
8. Hom 36; CS 123:313.
9. Timothy Fry, ed., *Rule of Saint Benedict 1980* (Collegeville, MN: Liturgical Press, 1980), 161.

God himself is "my holy Delight [*dulcedo mea sancta*]," cries Saint Augustine.[10] Elsewhere he associates sweetness particularly with the Holy Spirit, who is "the sweetness of the Begetter and the Begotten."[11] And looking at the cross of Christ with a poet's eye, contemplating the great work accomplished by it, Venantius Fortunatus exclaims: "Sweet the nails and sweet the wood, laden with so sweet a load" [*dulce ferrum, dulce lignum, dulce pondus sustinent*]."[12]

The patristic authors continue to use honey as a term of comparison; for Augustine it is wisdom, "holding the first place for sweetness among the viands of the heart";[13] for Gregory the Great, "to find honey (Pr 25:11) is to savor the sweetness of a holy thought."[14] In another interpretation, he compares honey, which falls from on high, to the knowledge of Christ's divinity, and butter, made from the milk of animals, to the mystery of his Incarnation.[15] Gregory warns that the devil offers a taste of his own kind of sweetness [*gustum suae dulcedinis*]: pride, avarice, envy, deceit, lust, so many beverages of his sweetness.[16]

More frequently, Gregory describes the contemplative experience as one of inner sweetness [*dulcedinem suavitatis aeternae*].[17] Again: "Sometimes one is admitted to a particular, unaccustomed experience of inner sweetness and, for a moment, he is, in some way, a new man, set afire by the breath of the Spirit. And the more he tastes the object of his love, the stronger grows his desire for it."[18]

10. Conf 1.4.22; *Conf* I/I:41.
11. De Trin 6.10.11; FC 45:214. This will be taken up by William of Saint-Thierry, and Saint Bernard uses a similar expression.
12. *Pange Lingua Gloriosi*, hymn for Passiontide, Cistercian breviary.
13. En in Ps 30.21; *Psalms* III/18:352.
14. Mo 16.8; SCh 221:149.
15. Mo 15.20; SCh 221:42.
16. Mo 15.71; SCh 221:128.
17. Hiez 1.5.12; Gray 51.
18. Mo 23.43; CF 77:122, n. 214.

* * *

In the light of this tradition, it is not surprising that the early Cistercians had a particular attraction to the *dulcedo Dei*. In the writings of Saint Bernard (known as the mellifluous doctor) we can see the diversity of objects which could be known as *dulcis* or *suavis*. All sweetness has its source in God; Bernard speaks of "the sweet name of Father"[19] and "the unimaginable sweetness of the Word,"[20] and calls the Holy Spirit "the very sweetness of God [*dulcissimum quiddam in Deo*]."[21] It is "with all the skill and sweetness of his divine artistry" that the Spirit accomplishes his work in our inmost being."[22]

Wise psychologist that he is, Bernard knows that the sweetness of Christ's humanity is necessary for beginners who are not able to perceive the things which are of the Spirit of God (1 Cor 2:14); he writes: "affection for Christ opposes the sweet enticements of sensual life. Sweetness conquers sweetness as one nail drives out another."[23] Without it the monastic life is dry and wearisome.[24] But this sweetness is not yet that experienced by the soul which has become bride, and is sweetly at rest in the delight of love [*amor suavitatem*][25] indeed "enraptured by the unutterable sweetness of the Word."[26] Even this sweetness will only come to perfection in heaven, which is, among other things, "a place of sweetness, where the Lord sweetly makes his presence known to all."[27]

God also communicates his sweetness to humans; for example: "The pastors and teachers appointed for men . . . ought

19. SC 15.2; CF 4:106.
20. SC 85.13; CF 40:209.
21. Pent 1.1; CF 53:69.
22. SC 17.2; CF 4:127.
23. SC 20.4; CF 4:150.
24. SC 9.2-3; CF 4:54-55.
25. SC 48.8; CF 31:20.
26. SC 85.13; CF 40:209.
27. Div 42.7; SBOp 6a:260.

to be sweet, that they may receive me with kindness and compassion. . . . Where can you find greater sweetness than that shown by Peter, who with infinite sweetness invited all sinners to come to him. . . . Most gladly shall I follow Paul who, in the excess of his sweetness, wept over those who had sinned and had done no penance."[28] In a similar vein, William of Saint-Thierry says that as the soul "tastes and sees how sweet the Lord is (Ps 33:9), all of a sudden its whole being grows sweet in tasting of his sweetness."[29] Later, he writes: "When you say to the longing soul 'Open your mouth wide and I will fill it' and she tastes and sees your sweetness, in the great Sacrament which surpasses understanding, then she is made that which she eats."[30] Longing for even more of this sweetness, William prays: "O good Father, loving Brother, and sweet Lord, you are all that is good and sweet and loving; the sum of goodness overflows in you. Open yourself to us, that your sweetness may flow forth from you to us, and fill us."[31]

The one who, above all others, was filled with the sweetness of God, was the Virgin Mary. Saint Ælred, contemplating her at the moment of the Incarnation, addresses her: "O sweet Lady, with what sweetness you were inebriated, with what a fire of love you were inflamed . . . when he took flesh to himself from your flesh."[32]

The Incarnate Word communicates his sweetness to those who contemplate him; thus Guerric of Igny finds in the child Jesus "all that is sweet and desirable . . . it is sweet to think and think again of this Child-God, sweet and utterly delicious . . . for him to be in us is a most effective remedy for curing and sweetening our rancor of soul, bitterness of speech and harshness of manners."[33] Ælred invites the recluse whom he is addressing to claim for herself "some portion of the sweetness" which the apostle John, leaning

28. PP 1.2; CF 53:101.
29. Med 3.12; CF 3:109.
30. Med 8.5; CF 3:142.
31. Med 6.12; CF 3:132.
32. Inst incl 26; CF 2:73.
33. Nat 1.4; CF 8:41.

on the breast of Jesus at the Last Supper, imbibed from "the honeycomb of eternal sweetness," either "the wine of gladness in the knowledge of the Godhead or, if she is not capable of that, "the milk which flows from Christ's humanity."[34]

Ælred speaks also of "the pleasantness of prayer . . . the sweetness of utterly grace-filled compunction . . . the sweetness of Christ's presence"[35] although he admits that "the sweetness of God that we taste in this life is given us not so much for enjoyment as for a consolation and encouragement for our weakness."[36] Love is "the heart's palate which tastes that [God] is sweet."[37] Besides divine sweetness there is that of brotherly love.[38] He notes that sweetness is not a sufficient motive for loving others, but when added to reason it perfects love.[39] While Ælred feels the need to pray "Lord, let but a drop of your surpassing sweetness fall upon my soul, that by it the bread of her bitterness may become sweet,"[40] Gilbert of Hoyland eulogizes him (Ælred) thus: "how great a honeycomb, how vast and how rich . . . his speech like a honeycomb poured out honeyed knowledge."[41]

Gilbert, indeed, never tires of speaking of sweetness, of honey and the honeycomb. In Sermon 31 he contrasts what is bitter and harsh—the wine of austerity, the word of the law, the heresies of Novatian and Pelagius—with the sweetness of the milk of consolation, the word of the Gospel, and the pardon and grace it brings, all of which are summed up in the new commandment of charity, "his ever fresh sweetness."

"Love," he adds, "cannot exist and fail to be sweet [*non potest amor esse, et dulcis non esse*]."[42] "Both are yours, good Jesus, the

34. Inst incl 31; CF 2:87.
35. Spec car 3.37.102; CF 17:293-4.
36. Spec car 3.39:108; CF 17:298.
37. Spec car 1.1.2; CF 17:88.
38. Spec car 3.2.5; CF 17:224; 3.4.7; 226; 3:4:12; 229.
39. Spec car 3.20.48; CF 17:254.
40. Spec car 1.1.2; CF 17:88.
41. S 41.4-6; CF 26:495-7.
42. S 31.5: CF 20:379-380.

honey you give and the honey you are";[43] "'How sweet is the Lord' (Ps 34:9). For what but the Lord is sweet?";[44] "How great is the extent of this sweetness (Ps 30:20), which you consider must be hidden, as long as you do not explain it! Whatever it is, it lies hidden within; but from these hidden recesses breathes the sweetest fragrance. Somehow while I guess that it is wonderfully sweet, I already sense that it is wonderfully sweet";[45] "Truly 'great is the wealth of your sweetness, O Lord, which you have hidden from those who fear you,' but not from those who love you."[46] His bride, the Church, shares his sweetness: "on the lips of the bride is only sweetness and full sweetness and measured sweetness."[47]

In a more philosophical mood, Gilbert muses on Joel 3:18, "the mountains will distill sweetness":

> Though "to distill" suggests the limitation of one drop at a time, still the abstract word, "sweetness," directs us beyond any limitation. Indeed, what else but infinity is expressed by an unending distillation? The more this unlimited sweetness is free from the limitation of any specific quality, the more it surpasses every limited sweetness. "The mountains will distill sweetness," says Joel, "and the hills will flow with milk." Though milk is sweet, milk is not sweetness itself. Sweetness is not only sweet but also sweetness itself, and from sweetness all things sweet are sweet, however different they be in kinds of sweetness, however differentiated they be in degrees of sweetness. Now whatever is sweet by participation in sweetness, still is not sweet by comparison with sweetness itself. Wherefore sweetness itself is not qualified, but stands alone in its simplicity, in order that the immensity of its reality may be linked with the very use of that word.[48]

---

43. S 40.8; CF 26:486.
44. Amp 2; CF 34:95.
45. S 22.4; CF 20:278.
46. S 25.5; CF 20:311.
47. S 35.2; CF 20:278.
48. Redemp; CF 34:48-49.

The author of the hymn *Jesu Dulcis Memoria*, thought to be an English Cistercian,[49] weaves the sweetness of Jesus in and out of his poem:

Jesu dulcis memoria,
Dans vera cordi gaudia:
Sed super mel et omnia
Ejus dulcis praesentia.

Nil canitur suavis . . .
Quam Jesus Dei Filius.[50]

Jesus is *dulcedo ineffabilis, dulcedo cordium, amor nostrae dulcedinis*; finally, in terms borrowed from Saint Bernard,[51] he is

Jesu decus Angelicum,
In aure dulce canticum,
In ore mel mirificum,
In corde nectar coelicum.[52]

Hardly less lyrical is the litany with which Baldwin of Forde ends his treatise *On the Sacrament of the Altar*: "Jesus is sweet, his name is sweet, his memory is the desire of the soul . . . he is sweet in prayer, in speech, in reading, in contemplation, in compunction, in the heart's jubilation. Sweet in the mouth, in the heart, in love; [*amor ipse dulcedinis et dulcedo amoris*]. . . . His inestimable sweetness is the first of his gifts and the greatest of his delights."[53]

49. "Jesu Dulcis Memoria," *New Catholic Encyclopaedia* (New York: McGraw-Hill, 1967), 7:892.

50. The sweet remembrance of Jesus gives the heart true joy, but beyond honey and all else is his sweet presence. . . . Nothing can more sweetly be sung than Jesus the Son of God.

51. SC 15.6; CF 4:110.

52. Jesus, delight of the angels, is a sweet song in the ear, wonderful honey in the mouth, heavenly nectar in the heart.

53. Sacr Altaris 3.2; SCh 94:566-9.

Chapter 11

GOING BEYOND ONESELF

Excessus mentis and *raptus*

One of the deepest yearnings of the human heart is the desire to go beyond oneself, to transcend one's normal, everyday limitations: physical, psychological and spiritual. Pascal expresses this longing in his famous phrase, "man infinitely surpasses man." It is this tendency to which Viktor Frankl also refers: "Human existence is essentially self-transcendence."[1] The early Cistercians, following their predecessors, express this desire by the terms *excessus mentis* and *raptus*. However, as is the case with other Latin words, if we are to understand their meaning in the tradition, we must put aside the overtones of their English counterparts, "ecstasy" and "rapture."

Going out of oneself, beyond oneself, is necessarily, inherently ambiguous: in what direction does one go? Toward fear, awe in the presence of the unknown, the numinous? Toward illusion, derangement, madness—literally going out of one's mind? Or toward transcendence, a profound experience of the divine? *Excessus*, like its Greek counterpart *ekstasis*, can bear any of the three meanings. To the extent that it points to this last meaning it merits to be called ecstasy in the strict sense.

---

1. *Man's Search for Meaning* (New York: Washington Square Press, 1963), 175. Frankl contrasts this with self-actualization which, he says, cannot be the real aim of human existence as it "is not a possible aim at all, for the simple reason that the more a man would strive for it, the more he would miss it. For only to the extent to which man commits himself to the fulfillment of his life's meaning, to this extent he also actualizes himself."

Raptus comes from the verb *rapere* whose basic meaning is to snatch, implying a certain violence; it is used for theft and rape. It is only when the "theological passive" is used, when God does the snatching, that it becomes a rapture.

The Bible has many ways to express the reality underlying the words *excessus* and *raptus*. The history of Israel begins with Abraham leaving his father's house "for the land I will show you" (Gen 12:1). Later the people make their archetypal journey from Egypt to the Promised Land. Even after they have been established in it, they continue to look forward to something beyond, whether it is expressed in messianic, apocalyptic or eschatological terms. The psalmists have their own, very personal way of expressing their yearning to go beyond themselves, into the sphere of the divine: "God will ransom me from death and take me to himself" (Ps 48:16); "You take hold of my right hand, you will lead me and receive me in your glory" (Ps 72:24). For the community, this yearning found expression in its worship and praise of Yahweh. Thus the whole thrust of the Old Testament is such that it can even be said that "Israel exists in a state of being taken outside itself."[2]

The same can be said of the New Testament. Jesus speaks of the mysterious kingdom of heaven, at hand and yet to come. Paul forgets what is behind and strains forward to what lies ahead; he longs to know as he is known. The letter to the Hebrews looks forward to the city that is to come, the book of Revelation to a new heaven and a new earth.

The biblical vocabulary is varied and fluid, and there is no consistency among the Hebrew, Greek and Latin versions. For *excessus*, the basic texts taken up by the tradition are Psalm 30:23 and Psalm 115:11. This was due in great part to the translators' decision to use *ekstasis* in the Septuagint and *excessus* in the Vulgate for the Hebrew *chaphaz*. This opened the way to an interpretation of the phrase *in excessus mentis* as ecstasy proper rather

2. Hans Urs von Balthasar, *The Glory of the Lord* (San Francisco: Ignatius, 1991) 5:179.

than the great fear implied by the Hebrew. *Excessus* is also used in Psalm 67:28, but in this case it is the result of a curious mistranslation of the Hebrew *radah*: "Benjamin their leader" becomes "Benjamin in ecstasy of mind."

Besides these psalm verses, it was especially two verses of Saint Paul's *Second Letter to the Corinthians* that the tradition mulled over, coaxed meaning out of, adapted to its own purposes. In chapter 12, Paul speaks of having been "caught up [*harpagenta*, Vulg *raptum*] to the third heaven." Significantly, "it is not the Apostle as such who was caught up in ecstasy, nor the member of some class of privileged beings, but 'a man in Christ.' From the time of the Ascension, humanity, made into a new creation by baptism, is on the way to the Kingdom where the glory of God will be made known: in exceptional cases, a partial revelation of this glory is granted."[3] In the second verse, 2 Corinthians 5:13, suddenly, enigmatically, with little relation to the preceding or following context, Paul writes tersely: "If we were beside ourselves [*exestemen*, Vulg *mente excedimus*], to God; if we were sober [*sophronoumev, sobrii*], to you." Paul seems to imply that sobriety and reasonableness are appropriate when relating to humans, but not when it is a matter of relating to the limitless, transcendent God.

In the tradition, Paul's *excessus* evoked the three psalm verses, especially Psalm 67:28, since Paul was of the tribe of Benjamin. The *raptus* of 2 Corinthians 12:2 became associated with Genesis 5:24 ("Enoch was seen no more, because God took him") and 2 Kings 2:3, 11 ("Elijah went up by a whirlwind into heaven"), even though different words are used. Paul's became the third archetypal rapture.

It is noteworthy that ecstasy is not used in the gospels with regard to Jesus, even in the theophanies of the Baptism and Transfiguration; nor is it used for the Resurrection appearances. The early Church, however, according to Luke's description in the Acts of the Apostles, was marked by a strongly ecstatic character

3. DSp 4:2085.

from its beginning. Luke interprets the Pentecost event as the fulfillment not only of the passage that he quotes (Joel 3:1-5), but of the whole prophetic and ecstatic tradition of the Old Testament, from the time of Moses (Num 11:10, 12:6) through the charismatic judges, Samuel, the brotherhoods of prophets, Elijah, Elisha, and the classical, writing prophets. Pentecost is the day foretold "when all the people, transformed by the experience of ecstasy, would be able to enter directly into relationship with YHWH, previously the privilege of the prophets."[4] Throughout Acts, Luke continues to give instances of ecstasy and rapture: the communal ecstasy of 4:31; Stephen's vision of 6:15 and 7:55-56; the ecstasy of Peter at Joppa (10:10) and that of Paul in the temple (22:17).

* * *

Besides its use in the Bible, ecstasy had a place in Hellenistic culture. As this has implications for its use in early Christian literature, some mention of it must be made here. A basic factor in Greek religion, *ekstasis'* Sitz im Leben was the cult of Dionysius/Bacchus—which tended to wild behavior, frenzy and various excesses. On the other hand, Greek philosophers too make use of the word *ekstasis*. Plato, for example, describes poets (none too flatteringly) as

> inspired and possessed . . . they are not in their right mind when they make their beautiful songs, but they are like Corybants out of their wits. As soon as they mount on their harmony and rhythm, they become frantic and possessed.[5]

Plotinus claims to have experienced ecstasy: "Often have I woken up out of the body to myself and entered into myself, going out from all other things."[6]

---

4. DSp 4:2087.

5. *Ion* 533; trans. W. H. D. Rouse (New York: New American Library, 1956), 18.

6. *Ennead* 4.8.1, quoted in Bernard McGinn, *The Foundations of Mysticism* (New York: Crossroad, 1992), 44.

In the writings of Philo of Alexandria, who drew on both Jewish and Greek tradition and tried to unite them, ecstasy holds an important place. A key text of Philo distinguishes four types of ecstasy. The terms he uses to describe them will be taken up by Christian authors:

> Now there is one kind of trance which is a sort of frantic delirium, causing infirmity of mind. . . . There is another kind which is excessive consternation, arising usually from things which happen suddenly and unexpectedly. Another kind is mere tranquillity of the mind, arising when it is inclined by nature to be quiet; but that which is the best description of all is a divinely inspired and more vehement sort of enthusiasm.[7]

Earlier in the same text he writes:

> Who, then, shall be the heir? Not that reasoning which remains in the prison of the body according to its own voluntary intentions, but that which is loosened from those bonds and emancipated, and which has advanced beyond the walls, and if it is possible to say so, has itself forsaken itself. "For he," says the Scripture, "who shall come out from thee, he shall be thy heir." Therefore if any desire comes upon thee, O soul, to be the inheritor of the good things of God, leave not only thy country, thy body, and thy kindred, the outward senses, and thy father's house, that is speech; but also flee from thyself, and depart out of thyself. . . . For while the mind is in a state of enthusiastic inspiration, and while it is no longer mistress of itself, but is agitated and drawn into frenzy by heavenly love, and drawn upwards to that object, truth removing all impediments out of its way, and making everything before it plain, that so it may advance by a level and easy road, its destiny is to become an inheritor of the things of God.[8]

---

7. *Quis rerum divinarum heres sit* 249; *Philo*, trans. C. D. Yonge (Peabody, MA: Hendrickson, 1993), 297.

8. Quis rerum, 68-70; 281.

This philosophical tradition facilitated the acceptance of *ekstasis* into the Christian vocabulary.

There is little reference to mysticism in early Christian literature and even less mention of *ekstasis*. In the early Church, ecstasy was lived rather than expressed, and communal rather than individual: an experience of being in Christ, in the Spirit. There is a connection between *ekstasis* and prophetic revelation;[9] indeed, a direct line from prophecy to the gift of the Spirit. In Saint Irenaeus' words: "Where the Church is, there is the Spirit of God; and where the Spirit of God is, there is the Church and every kind of grace"[10]—including vision, contemplation and ecstasy.

Often, however, *ekstasis* is used in an unfavorable sense. It is associated with the Delphic oracle—whose priestess is driven "into such a state of ecstasy and madness [*ekstasin kai maniken*] that she loses control of herself"[11]—and with fringe groups that border on heresy like the Montanists. Eusebius describes Montanus in this way: "in his unbridled ambition to reach the top . . . he was filled with spiritual excitement and suddenly fell into a kind of trance and unnatural ecstasy. He raved and began to chatter and talk nonsense."[12] In Origen's view, such ecstasies are something to be removed by invoking the name of Jesus.[13]

According to Saint Jerome,[14] Tertullian, when he had become associated with the Montanists, wrote a treatise in six books *De ecstasi*. This work is no longer extant, but Tertullian elsewhere describes at some length a member of his congregation "favored with sundry gifts of revelation, which she experiences in the

9. Justin, *Dialogue with Trypho* 115; ANF 1:256; Athenagoras, *A Plea for the Christians* 9: ANF 2:132; Tertullian, *De anima* 11: ANF 3:191.

10. Irenaeus, Adv her 3.24.1; ANF 1:458.

11. Origen, *Contra Celsum* 7.3; ANF 4:612.

12. *Ecclesiastical History*, trans. G. A. Williamson (New York: Dorset Press, 1965), 218.

13. *Contra Celsum* 1.67; ANF 4:427.

14. *De viris illustribus* 25, 40, 53; PL 23:644, 656, 664.

Spirit by ecstatic vision."[15] Extravagant overtones of this sort made "ecstasy" suspect in the mainline church.

In spite of the avoidance of the term, the reality expressed by *ekstasis* is present in Christian spiritual writers. Though he avoids the term, Clement of Alexandria's mysticism can certainly be called ecstatic, "since his *gnosis* is an incessant, ceaseless search, which can only be concluded by an encounter with the one who is sought, to be united with him in love."[16] Origen seldom mentions *ekstasis*, but the concept of continually going beyond oneself is basic to his thought. "There is no end to the task of those who labor for wisdom and knowledge. Indeed the more one enters into God's wisdom, the deeper one goes, and the more one investigates, the more inexpressible and inconceivable it becomes."[17] For Origen, every "going up" mentioned in the Bible symbolizes a spiritual ascent.[18] This is true especially for the journey of the Israelites from Egypt to the promised land as recounted in the book of Numbers.[19]

It is Gregory of Nyssa who, more than anyone, can be said to have "Christianized" *ekstasis*. The development of the theology of transcendence in the fourth century made possible a more exact formulation of an experience which earlier writers, because of a lack of proper vocabulary, were unable to express clearly.[20] Doubtless also the Dionysian and Montanist overtones of the word had waned by then. For Gregory, ecstasy is an experience of the transcendence of God that takes the soul out if itself. It is not irrational, but suprarational. Furthermore, the Christian life itself is a ceaseless ecstasy to the extent that it is an approach to the mystery of creation and redemption. For the created being, "to be" means "to be outside oneself."[21]

15. *De anima* 9; ANF 3:188.

16. DSp 4: 2093.

17. In Num hom 17.4; *Origen: Spirit and Fire* by Hans Urs von Balthasar (Washington, DC: Catholic UP, 1984), 25 (hereafter, Origen).

18. For example, Rebecca: *In Gen hom* 12.2; FC 71:177-8.

19. In Num hom 27.4-12; Origen, 68-72.

20. "Contemplation," DSp 2:1876.

21. "Exstase." DSp 2099.

This concept of ecstasy as a tendency rather than a fleeting experience appears also in Saint John Climacus. In his book *The Ladder of Divine Ascent*, whose very title is evocative, he describes a monk as "a perpetual ecstasy and mourning of life."[22] The early monks were generally reticent when it came to describing their experiences of the transcendent. Yet we do find *ekstasis/excessus mentis* in their *Sayings* and *Lives* which have come down to us. Although it is not used frequently, when it does occur—often in conjunction with *harpagenta/raptus*—it is without comment, explanation or elaboration; almost matter-of-factly. It nearly always refers to a vision, and is an experience which has nothing to do with the holiness of the visionary; indeed, it is often an admonition or warning to inspire a tepid monk to conversion.[23] Occasionally it means something more profound, as for example:

> At one time Zachary went to his abbot Silvanus, and found him in an ecstasy [*in excessu mentis*], and his hands were stretched out to heaven. And when he saw him thus, he closed the door and went away: and coming back about the sixth hour, and the ninth, he found him even so: but toward the tenth hour he knocked, and coming in found him lying quiet and said to him, "What ailed thee today, Father?" And he said, "I was ill today, my son." But the young man held his feet saying, "I shall not let thee go, until thou tell me what thou hast seen." The old man answered him: "I was caught up [*raptus*] into heaven, and I saw the glory of God. And I stood there until now, and now am I sent away."[24]

22. Trans. Colm Luibheid and Norman Russell (New York: Paulist, 1982), 209.

23. For example, *Vitae Patrum* 5.3.20, 5.11.8; *Western Asceticism*, trans. Owen Chadwick (Philadelphia: Westminster, 1958), 47, 104.

24. *Vitae Patrum* 6.1.1; *The Desert Fathers*, trans. Helen Waddell (Ann Arbor, MI: U of Michigan Press, 1957), 125–26. See also *Apophthegma Patrum*, Poemen 144; PL 65:358; *Vitae Patrum* 5.12.11; *Western Asceticism* 143.

The father of monks, Saint Anthony of the desert, had such experiences[25] and his biographer, Saint Athanasius, gives an interesting description of one of them: "He felt himself carried off [*harpagenta*], in thought, and the wonder was that while he was standing there he saw himself as if he were outside himself."[26]

In his *Confessions*, Saint Augustine twice speaks of rapture. Even before his conversion, he was ravished to God by God's beauty, but was unable to sustain the experience.[27] Later, he describes his last conversation with Monica at Ostia and their ascent toward God, beyond all creatures, beyond their very souls, until, while "talking of God's wisdom and panting for it, with all the efforts of their hearts they did for one instant attain to touch it." He concludes that if "this could continue . . . and so ravish and absorb and wrap the beholder in inward joys that his life should eternally be such as that one moment of understanding . . . would not this be: 'enter into the joy of your Lord.'"[28]

Augustine equates *ecstasis* and *excessus mentis*.[29] When he comments on the psalms in which *excessus mentis* appears, he stresses the same elements as in the *raptus* of the *Confessions*: the experience is ineffable—*nescio quid*, he says again and again—and it does not last. Typical is this passage from his *Commentary on Psalm 37*:

> This is what has happened. In a transport of soul he has beheld something indescribably sublime, but was not yet wholly lost in what he saw. A kind of lightning flash, if it may be so termed, of light eternal lit up the scene, so to speak, and made him feel that he had not yet attained to it. . . . Such is the ineffable vision seen in ecstasy, that it makes me realize how far off I am, who have not yet attained to it.[30]

25. *The Life of Anthony*, trans. Robert C. Gregg (New York: Paulist, 1980), 90.

26. Ibid., 78–79.

27. Conf 7.17; *Conf* 176-8.

28. Conf 9.10.23-5; *Conf* I/I:26-9.

29. En in Ps 34 2.6; *Psalms* III/16:64-5.

30. En in Ps 37.12; *Psalms* III/16:155-6. The fullest explanation is in En in Ps 30.1-2; *Psalms* III/15:321-4. See also En in Ps 115.3; *Psalms* III/19:328, S 52.16; *Sermons* 3:57; Ep 147.31; FC 20:199.

For Cassian *excessus mentis* is due to "a visit of the Holy Spirit, a sudden illumination bringing ineffable joy of heart"[31] and not due to one's own merits.[32] Yet it is also the true perfection of the third renunciation when "by constant meditation on things divine and spiritual contemplation [the soul] has so far passed on to things unseen, that it . . . is caught up into such an ecstasy" as not to hear or see what is before it.[33] Cassian looks at it as occurring more frequently in the eremitical life. Abbot John recalls how "I have often been enraptured in such transports that I forgot the burden of this fragile body. . . . I thought of God and contemplation filled my heart."[34]

For cenobites it is more likely to occur during the profound silence and recollection of the night office[35] or when the soul is moved to thanksgiving by the memory of God's past kindnesses.[36] Above all, it is at the heart of what Cassian calls pure prayer—the prayer that "centers on no contemplation of some image or other, and is marked by no attendant sounds or words. It is a fiery outbreak, an indescribable exaltation, an insatiable thrust of the soul. Free of what is sensed and seen, ineffable in its groans and sighs, the soul pours itself out to God."[37]

In his "little rule, written for beginners" (RB 73:8), Saint Benedict does not mention *excessus* or *raptus*. Perhaps he hints at them when speaking of "our hearts overflowing with the inexpressible delight of love" (RB Prol. 49). Yet he is continually inviting his disciples to go beyond themselves, to run in the way of God's commandments while they have the light of life (RB Prol. 49, 9), to hasten to the perfection of monastic life (RB 73:2), to their heavenly home (RB 73:8), to the eternal life that they are to desire with

31. Conl 10.10.12; Ramsey 382.

32. Conl 4.5; Ramsey 157. See also Conl 6.10.2; Ramsey 225.

33. Conl 3.7.3; Ramsey 125. See also Conl 9.15.1; Ramsey 338 and Conl 12.12.7; Ramsey 451.

34. Conl 19.4.1; Ramsey 671.

35. Inst 2.10.1; SCh 109:74; NPF 11:209.

36. Conl 9.14; Ramsey 338.

37. Conl 10.11.9; Ramsey 385.

all the passion of the soul (RB 4:45), to climb the ladder of humility which will lead them to perfect love (RB 7:5, 67).

Benedict himself, according to his biographer Saint Gregory the Great, knew *excessus* and *raptus* by experience. Gregory stresses that from his youth Benedict lived with himself [*secum*], "at all times keeping close watch over his life and actions," rather than living away from himself [*extra se*], or below himself [*sub se*]. Already at that stage of his spiritual growth, "each time that the ardor of his contemplation snatched him to the heights, he was raised above himself [*super se*]."[38] Later, toward the end of his life, in what Gregory sees as the culmination of his spiritual ascent, Benedict saw "the whole world gathered up before his eyes in what appeared to be a single ray of light." Gregory goes on to explain:

> The light of holy contemplation enlarges and expands the mind in God until it stands above the world. In fact, the soul that sees him rises even above itself [*super semetipsam*]. . . . Absorbed as [Benedict] was in God, it was now easy for him to see all that lay beneath God. In the light outside that was shining before his eyes, there was a brightness which reached into his mind and lifted his spirit heavenward, showing him the insignificance of all that lies below.[39]

Gregory points out a kind of paradox with regard to ecstasy. "After hard labors, after floods of temptation, the soul is often suspended in ecstasy;"[40] yet "the person who is most carried away in contemplation is most bothered by temptation."[41] Another paradox: in Mor 23:21:41, Gregory writes, "being raised up in ecstasy, which our interpreters improperly [*non proprie*] call fear."[42] Some manuscripts omit the *non*; is it proper or not to equate ecstasy and fear?

38. Di 2.3.5-9; FC 39:62-3.
39. Di 2.35:3-7; FC 39:105-6.
40. Mor 24.6.12; CC 143B:1196.
41. Robert Gillet, Introduction, Grégoire le Grand, *Morales sur Job*, SCh 32:59.
42. PL 76:276.

* * *

Among the Cistercians, it is Saint Bernard who has the most to say about *excessus* and *raptus*. Jean Leclercq explains how important they are in Bernard's thought:

> All of Bernard's teaching is concerned with the passage from "flesh" to "spirit" in the Pauline sense, and from self-centeredness to an openness to the whole of creation as a result of going beyond oneself, of surpassing that instinctive self, as yet unliberated by grace. In its most elevated forms, this going beyond will be the *excessus* or going out of self that is ecstasy. But apart from these exceptional cases, those rare, brief moments, the monk, who performs the duties incumbent on every Christian with total dedication, must try each day to surpass himself, to raise himself to the level of the grace that is already present and active in him.[43]

Bernard looks at *excessus* from different perspectives. The whole thrust of his early work *The Steps of Humility* is a double *excessus*. This is *excessus mentis* as a tendency rather than a fleeting experience. It presupposes a prior step: the "return to the heart" that Bernard so often speaks of. There one learns the first step of truth, the truth about oneself: one's contingency, mortality, neediness. Once this is accepted, one can proceed to the first *excessus*. This is not yet to contemplation of the Truth that is God, but a necessary preliminary: to knowledge of one's neighbor. Bernard explains this by means of Psalm 115:10-11:

> "I was humbled exceedingly:" in my own eyes, I fell very low. . . . Up to this he has been examining himself. Now he looks out from himself to others and thus passes to the second step of truth, exclaiming in his *excessus*, "every man is a liar." What is meant by "in his excess"? It means that he was carried away by feelings of mercy and compassion.[44]

43. Introduction to *Bernard of Clairvaux: Selected Works*, trans. G. R. Evans (New York: Paulist, 1987), 38.
44. Hum 15-16; CF 13:44.

Bernard underlines the nature of the second step of truth by contrasting it with a very different kind of *excessus*: the conceit of the proud Pharisee who said in his excess, "I give you thanks, O God, that I am not like the rest of men"(Luke 18:11). After explaining how far from the truth the Pharisee was, Bernard cannot resist a play on still another meaning of the word *excessus*: "I am afraid I am speaking in my excess now myself and have wandered away from my subject. Still, no harm is done if I have conveyed to you the difference between the two kinds of 'excess.'"[45]

Bernard then returns to his subject. Having ascended to the first step of truth by the toil of humility and to the second by a deep feeling of compassion, we make the further ascent to the knowledge of God, truth in itself, by the *excessus* of contemplation. Here "pure truth sweeps us up to the sight of things invisible," "the hidden home of Truth itself." This is *excessus* in the more restricted sense; the third heaven to which Paul was caught up (2 Cor 12:4). Interestingly, it is the Father who thus exalts us.[46]

Bernard explains what he means by *excessus mentis* in one of the *Various Sermons*: "Sometimes the interior man exceeds reason and is snatched above himself."[47] He distinguishes two kinds of *excessus*: "One in the intellect, the other in the will; one of enlightenment, the other of fervor; one of knowledge, the other of devotion."[48] From another point of view, in the first we go beyond the desires of the flesh to purity of heart, and in the second, beyond images and ideas, to pure prayer.[49]

Even the angels experience *excessus* and *raptus*, particularly the Dominations and the Seraphim.[50] But Bernard holds these graces out to his monks as something they too may hope to ex-

---

45. Hum 17; CF 13:45.
46. Hum 19, 23; CF 13:47, 53.
47. Div 115; SBOp 6A:392.
48. SC 49.4; CF 31:24.
49. SC 52.4-5; CF 31:52-3. This seems to be a reminiscence of Cassian's second and third renunciations: Conl 3.10; Cassian 91-2.
50. SC 19.3-5; CF 4:142-3.

perience, provided they live their monastic life with fervor.[51] This will prepare them for "a flight made on the two wings of purity and ecstasy."[52] In this flight the spirit "is ravished out of itself and granted a vision of God that suddenly shines into the mind with the swiftness of a lightning flash."[53] "The soul leaves even its bodily senses . . . so that in her awareness of the Word she is not aware of herself. This happens when the mind is enraptured by the ineffable sweetness of the Word, so that it withdraws, or rather is transported, *rapitur*, and escapes from itself to enjoy the Word."[54]

Corresponding to the ascent of the purified soul, *excessus purae mentis*, to God, is the wondrous condescension of God's loving descent, *Dei pium decessum*, into the soul.[55] This evokes the whole economy of the Incarnation and Redemption. Taking up a traditional theme,[56] Bernard recalls that both Adam (Gen 2:21) and Christ on the cross slept, but while the cause of Adam's sleep was *excessus contemplationis*, that of Christ was *miserationis affectu*. "Truth cast the sleep upon the first Adam, and charity upon the second."[57]

Excessus is accomplished by love;[58] indeed, it is the fruit of the kiss of the mouth.[59] One who has experienced being caught up to the third heaven "finds a cross in everything to which the world is attached and attaches himself to whatever seems a cross to the world."[60] He may even "become capable of savoring something of the sweetness of heavenly bliss" and attain, at least fleetingly, to the third degree of freedom, freedom from sorrow.[61]

---

51. SC 13.7; CF 4:95.
52. Csi 5.5; CF 37:142.
53. SC 41.3; CF 7:207.
54. SC 85.13; CF 40:209.
55. SC 31.6; CF 7:129.
56. See Jean Daniélou, *From Shadows to Reality* (London: Burns and Oates, 1960), 48-56.
57. Sept 2.1; Luddy 2:63.
58. Ep 11.2; *Letters* 42.
59. SC 4.4; CF 4:23.
60. Quad 6.3; Luddy 2:110.
61. Gra 5.15; CF 19:71.

This is probably what Bernard means when he writes:

> Some are drawn (Sg 1:3) and some are led, and some also are rapt, as the Apostle was, rapt even to the third heaven. Blessed are they who belong [to the first and second category], but most blessed of all they of the third who, having buried, so to speak, their own power of free choice in the profound depths of the divine mercy, are rapt in fervor of spirit into the riches of his glory (Eph 3:16), not knowing whether they are in the body or out of the body, conscious of nothing save that they have been rapt.[62]

The other Cistercians add their own nuances to Bernard's descriptions. Saint Ælred, for example, speaks not of the three steps of truth, but of the three sabbaths: on the first the soul is recollected within itself, *colligitur ad se*; on the second it is extended outside itself, *extenditur extra se*; on the third it is caught up above itself, *rapitur extra se*.[63] Both Bernard and Ælred understand ecstasy as "an outward journey, beginning with the death of selfishness, moving through concern for others and a growing disinterested love for God to absorption in him in utter self-forgetfulness."[64]

We can catch a glimpse of the ecstatic experience from the attempts the Cistercians made to describe it. Baldwin of Forde believed, "In the rapture of contemplation, the unfathomable God is sought in an unfathomable way."[65] In ecstasy, William of Saint-Thierry asserts, "something loved rather than thought and tasted rather than understood grows sweet and ravishes the lover."[66] For Ælred, ecstasy may mean being caught up into a certainty regarding one's salvation.[67] In it, Isaac of Stella says, one becomes

62. Asc 2.6; Luddy 2:238-9.

63. Spec car 3.36.19; CF 17:234.

64. Michael Casey, "In Pursuit of Ecstasy," *Monastic Studies* 16 (Christmas 1985): 142.

65. Baldwin, S 12.16; CF 38:221.

66. William, Cant 99; CF 6:80.

67. Ælred, S 34.26; CCCM 2:285.

more than human.[68] What is revealed in *excessus mentis* can scarcely or not at all be spoken of afterwards.[69] Yet by means of it, John of Forde adds, Christ is fashioning the Bride's heart into that peace which surpasses all understanding (Phil 4:7).[70]

Excessus mentis is sometimes compared to sleep,[71] "a genuine sleep that yet does not stupefy the mind but transports it, *non sopiat, sed abducat*" in Bernard's words.[72] William describes it thus:

> In her transport and ecstasy [*in excessus suo seu exstasi*], in the slumber of quiet, the Bride hears the voice of him who entreats her; she feels the grace with which he inspires her and sees the power with which he works. . . . he discovers [to her] the thick woods of his mysteries (Ps 28:5).[73]

Gilbert of Hoyland, commenting on Song 5:2, has an interesting variation: "I sleep for my friend gives rest; I watch for he grants rapture."[74]

The ecstatic experience brings "a pleasant cloud of unawareness, . . . an enveloping mist of loving forgetfulness."[75] Those who are rapt in contemplation are inebriated with the wine that gladdens the heart of man (Ps 103:15).[76] John of Forde catches its ambiguity: "This cry ['I wished to be an anathema from Christ for my brethren' (Rom 9:3)] is the cry of a man who is intoxicated or of a soul taken up into ecstasy, not to say that of a madman."[77]

Recalling Paul's experience in 2 Corinthians 5:13, the authors bring out the contrast between his being transported to God, *mentis excedimus Deo*, and sober for the sake of others, *sobrii vobis*. These

---

68. Isaac, S 37.29; SCh 207:302.

69. Isaac, S 4.10; CF 11:32.

70. John of Forde, S 68.3; CF 45:80.

71. John of Forde, S 97.5; CF 46:181; Gilbert, S 14.1; CF 14:165.

72. Bernard SC 52.3; CF 31:52.

73. William, Cant 140; CF 6:112.

74. S 42.2; CF 26:505.

75. John of Forde, S 46.3; CF 43:193.

76. Ælred, S 26.36; CCCM 2:218.

77. S 72.3; CF 45:120.

"others" are usually thought to be the less advanced souls.[78] Gilbert expresses it beautifully:

> You see how with Paul [the Bride] either flies beyond reason for God or bends down for our sake. "Charity impels us," says Paul. (2 Co 5:14) To what does it impel us? To ecstasy? No, not to ascend in ecstasy but to descend in charity. The former is the object of aspiration but the latter of service.[79]

William, however, applies the sobriety to the Bride herself:

> When [the Bride] is transported in mind to God, following the Lamb wherever he goes (Rv 14:4), she offers her entire self in love; once she becomes sober, returning to herself, she must recollect her entire being in understanding and nourish her soul at leisure with the fruits of spiritual knowledge.[80]

Excessus mentis has its own dangers. "In the cellar of wine (Sg 1:3)," says William, "charity to such an extent grows impetuous, overflows in its excesses, and rejoices over what it longs for, that it seems to abandon order, unless it is set in order anew by the King (Sg 2:4)."[81] It is the function of discretion, John of Forde explains, "to define the exact amount of every single virtue, and it restrains within fixed limits the excesses and ardent impulses of charity itself."[82] This discretion

> keeps [the Bride], as it were, balanced in the middle, between both extremes, that is, ecstatic joy and grief, so that she falls into neither danger. If it goes well with her, she is not thereby made overconfident, and if it goes ill, not overfearful[83] . . . . She subdues the raptures of what she in-

78. Bernard, Div 87.2; SBOp 6A:330; William, Cant 137; CF 6:110; Ælred S 26.36; CCCM 2:218; John of Forde, S 39.3; CF 43:117-8.
79. S 31.1; CF 20:374.
80. Cant 46; CF 6:36; see also Cant 147; 526; 120.
81. Cant 117; CF 6:94.
82. S 77.9; CF 45:194. Compare Bernard, SC 49.5; CF 31:25.
83. John sees excesses of overflowing joy to be as dangerous as those of overwhelming fear: S 64.3; CF 45:16.

tensely experiences by a certain sedate restraint, so that when she is carried out of herself, *rapitur supra se,* she is not carried away from herself, *rapitur a se* more than is right. She can, therefore, leave herself to pass into her God, *excedit in Deum suum,* without forgetting her weight. She can concentrate with all her heart on what is here and now, without ceasing to think of what soon will be."[84]

William speaks for them all when he declares that no matter how sublime the experience of *excessus mentis* or *raptus* in this life, it is never wholly satisfying:

This embrace (Sg 2:6) is begun here, to be perfected elsewhere. . . . This ecstasy dreams of something far more than what it sees; this secret sighs for another secret; this joy evokes another joy; this sweetness foretells another sweetness.[85]

Isaac adds that only after the final *excessus* of death, when God will be completely turned toward us, and catch us up perfectly to himself, will we be completely happy.[86]

84. John of Forde, S 46.6; CF 43:197.
85. William, Cant 132; CF 6:106.
86. Isaac, S 34.28; SCh 207:252.

Chapter 12

DELIGHT IN THE LORD

Fruitio Dei

Enjoying God—we are meant to find our joy, our delight, our fulfillment in God. This conviction is a constant in Christian tradition. It is deeply rooted in the Bible: The Psalms invite us to rejoice and delight in the Lord (Ps 149:2; 36:4); Mary found joy in God her Savior (Luke 1:47); and Jesus speaks of entering the joy of the Lord (Matt 25:21; also John 14:28; 16:22, 24). The word *fruor* itself, however, is used in the Vulgate only with respect to worldly, even illicit joys.[1] The one apparent exception is Philemon 20: "May I enjoy you in the Lord," but here *fruor* is a translation of the Greek *onaimen*, which Paul uses as a play on the name Onesimus. This translation will have its influence on later writers, as we shall see.

Fruor as a technical term takes its origin from philosophers such as Varro,[2] who defines virtue as the ability to use things well; this good use consists in relating these things to the Supreme Good. *Fruor*, therefore, is to love and to seek a good for itself; *utor* is to relate one good to another.[3] Christian thinkers took over this distinction; Saint Augustine is the first Latin writer to make extended use of it.[4]

---

1. Eccl 2:10; 5:17; Prov 7:18; Wis 2:16.
2. Marcus Terentuis Varro, BC 116–27. Greatest of ancient Roman scholars (Saint Augustine called him "the acute and learned Varro, the master of history").
3. DSp 5:1546-59.
4. Saint Augustine's thought has been thoroughly studied by Oliver O'Donovan in "*Usus* and *Fruitio* in Augustine, *De doctrina Christiana I*," JTS 33 (1982): 361.

Augustine's explanation of *fruitio* is not altogether consistent. In the *Confessions* he speaks of enjoying God to some extent even before his conversion—but not in a stable or lasting way.[5] In other early works, God is not the only legitimate object of enjoyment, but also reason,[6] truth,[7] and the most blessed life.[8]

In the thirtieth of the *Eighty-Three Questions*, Augustine contrasts *frui* and *uti*: "Every human perversion consists in the desire to use what ought to be enjoyed and to enjoy what should be used."[9]

It is in *De doctrina christiana* that he expounds most fully on this contrast, giving this explanation of the two: "To enjoy something is to hold fast to it in love for its own sake. To use something is to apply whatever it may be to the purpose of obtaining what you love."[10]

And again:

> Those things which are to be enjoyed make us happy; those which are to be used assist us and give us a boost, so to speak, as we press on toward our happiness, so that we may reach and hold fast to the things which make us happy.[11]

Since God alone can make us happy, he concludes: "The things [*res*] which are to be enjoyed are the Father and the Son and the Holy Spirit, and the Trinity comprised by them, which is a kind of single, supreme thing, shared by all who enjoy it."[12] Logically, then, even other people and one's own self, are not to be loved for their own sake (that is, enjoyed), but only for the sake of him

5. Conf 7.17, 8.5; *Conf* I/I:176, 192.
6. C acad 1.8.23; PL 32:917.
7. Beat vita 4.35; FC 5:83.
8. Ord 1.8.24; PL 32:989.
9. Quæs ev 83.30; FC 70:56.
10. Doc chr 1.4.4; *De Doctrina Christiana*, trans. and ed. R. P. H. Green (Oxford: Clarendon, 1993), 15; hereafter, Green.
11. Doct chr 1.3.3; Green 15.
12. Doct chr 1.5.5; Green 17.

who is the true object of enjoyment (and hence used). Augustine does draw that conclusion:

> Only external and unchangeable things are to be enjoyed; other things are to be used so that we may attain the full enjoyment of those things. We ourselves who enjoy and use other things are things. A human being is an important kind of thing being made in the image and likeness of God. . . . It is therefore an important question, whether humans should enjoy one another or use one another, or both. We have been commanded to love one another, but the question is whether one person should be loved by another on his own account or for some other reason. If on his own account, we enjoy him; if for another reason, we use him. In my opinion, he should be loved for another reason.[13]

So love of others, which is right and proper, must be distinguished from enjoyment, which is, at least in Augustine's eyes, reserved for God.

This conclusion may seem to us too rigid and restrictive. Is there really no room for enjoying other people: one's friends for example, or one's beloved spouse? The explanation may be that *fruor* is a philosophical term, and that Augustine is writing as a philosopher and trying to fit everything into categories. He is also so convinced of the immeasurable difference between God and all other beings, and so aware of our basic orientation toward God that he is reluctant to ascribe any other object to *fruor*.[14]

It does not seem that Augustine himself was entirely comfortable with his conclusion; later in the same work, when he repeats that our supreme reward is fully to enjoy God, he adds that "all of us who enjoy God may enjoy one another in Him."[15]

---

13. Doc chr 1.22.20; Green 29.

14. Katherine M. TePas Yohe draws attention to a certain ambivalence in the Christian tradition with regard to human friendship and love, its roots going back to Scripture: "Spiritual Friendship in Ælred of Rievaulx and Mutual Sanctification in Marriage," CSQ 27 (1992): 63.

15. Doct chr 1.32.35; Green 45.

Yet even this concession is qualified; Paul's wish to enjoy Philemon in the Lord (Phlm 20) is a transferred [*abusive*] use of the word. "When you enjoy a human being in God, you are enjoying God rather than that human being."[16]

Finally in the same work he drops the term *usus* altogether and instead makes a distinction between *caritas* and *cupiditas*:

> By *caritas* I mean the impulse [*motum*] of one's mind to enjoy God on his own account and to enjoy oneself and one's neighbor on account of God [*propter Deum*]. By *cupiditas* I mean the impulse of one's mind to enjoy oneself and one's neighbor and any corporeal thing not on account of God [*non propter Deum*].[17]

This formulation seems to be a more satisfactory view of the matter.

Even *cupiditas*, however, can have a legitimate place: "Love yearning to possess the object loved is desire [*cupiditas*]; love delighting in [*frui*] the object possessed is joy."[18]

The difference between *fruitio* and *usus*, *cupiditas* and *desiderium* is closely bound up with the difference between our present state *in via* and our future state in eternity. Here

> we are but travelers on a journey without as yet a fixed abode; we are on our way, not yet in our native land; we are

16. Doct chr 1.33.37; Green 47. Green comments: "The distinctive analysis of love in terms of enjoyment and use was never repeated by Augustine, and in retrospect the book [*De Doctrina Christiana*] must be regarded as experimental and inconclusive."

17. Doc chr 3.10.16; Green 149. Augustine expands on this thought in *De Trinitate* 9.8.13; FC 45:282: "Desire [*cupiditas*] is present when the creature is loved on account of itself. Then it does not help him who uses it, but corrupts him who enjoys it. Since the creature is either equal or inferior to us, we must use the inferior for God and enjoy the equal, but in God. . . . Therefore, let us enjoy ourselves and our brethren in the Lord."

18. Civ Dei 14.7.2; FC 14:360.

in a state of longing but not yet of enjoyment [*"desideranda, nondum fruendo"*].[19]

Temporalities like money are needed, but they are "things which you employ for a need, not which you enjoy for delight."[20] As he says elsewhere, "Using things, after all, appears to be one thing, enjoying them another. I mean we use things out of necessity, we enjoy them for fun [*pro jucunditate*]. So [God] has given us these temporal things to use, himself to enjoy."[21] When we arrive at our destination and see God as he is (John 3:2), "we will have no other occupation than to praise God and enjoy him."[22]

* * *

The early Middle Ages continued to use *frui* and *fruitio* generally with respect to everlasting life. "Every soul that earnestly devotes itself through love to belonging for supreme blessedness, shall at some time receive that blessedness to enjoy," Saint Anselm declares in the *Monologion* and goes on to explain that in that state:

> It will be impossible to turn the soul aside by any fear, or to deceive it by false security; nor, having once received the need of that blessedness, will it be able not to love it; nor will that blessedness desert the soul that loves it; nor shall there be anything powerful enough to separate them against their will. Hence, the soul that has once begun to enjoy supreme blessedness will be eternally blessed.[23]

Indeed, the rational creature "was created for the purpose of being happy in the enjoyment of God."[24]

19. S 103.1; *Sermons* III/4:76.

20. In Ev Ioann 40.10; FC 88:133.

21. S 177.8; PL 38:958; *Sermons* 3/5:283.

22. En in Ps 86.9; *Psalms* III/18:255.

23. Mono 70; *Saint Anselm, Basic Writings*, trans. S. N. Deane (LaSalle, IL: Open Court Classics, 1962), 182–83; henceforth, Deane.

24. Cur 1.9; *Anselm of Canterbury*, ed. and trans. Jasper Hopkins and Herbert Richardson (Toronto and New York: Edwin Mellen, 1974–76), 3:61.

In the *Proslogion* Anselm asks: "He who would enjoy this good, what will be his and what will not be his?" and proceeds to answer his own question: "He will have whatever he wants, and what he does not want he will not have."[25]

A different side of Anselm comes out in his "Meditation on the Passion of Christ," where he imagines Christ on the Cross saying:

> O my beloved, how often you have desired to enjoy the kiss of my mouth, saying to my companions, "Let him kiss me with the kiss of his mouth" (Sg 1.1). I am ready, my head inclined, my mouth open, to be kissed as much as you like. Do not say in your heart, "This kiss, without beauty or comeliness (Is 53.2), is not the one I seek, but that glorious one which the citizens of heaven long to enjoy." Do not err, because unless this mouth is first kissed, you will not attain to the other kiss.[26]

This more affective, even mystical use of *frui* would be developed by writers of the Middle Ages, including the Cistercians.

* * *

The early Cistercians in general are sparing in their use of *frui* and *fruitio*, although they extend its meaning in some interesting ways, while continuing to be influenced by the Augustinian tradition. Guerric of Igny, for instance, contrasts *uti* and *frui*:

> Do not they truly possess all things, if they have God for their portion (Ps 118:57) and inheritance (Nb 18:20), and possess Him who contains all things and disposes of them all? This is the God who, lest there be anything lacking to those who fear Him (Ps 33:10), gives to them for their use all things outside Himself, in the measure that He knows is good for them, and keeps Himself for their enjoyment. When the heir of God and the coheir with Christ (Rm 8:17)

25. Pros 25; Deane 76.
26. Med 10; PL 158:761.

comes of age and is set free from all restrictions, and so
enters into the full possession of the longed-for inheritance,
he will then be given an absolute rule and a free sway over
all creatures. . . . Even now, however, the world is full of
riches for the man of faith. He makes use of them to help
him to know and love their Creator, treating them as if they
had been given him for this precise purpose.[27]

The Cistercians acknowledge that only in heaven will there be
full fruition of God, when, as Guerric says, "faith will be transformed into knowledge, hope into possession, desire into
enjoyment."[28] But even in this life, they are convinced, a certain
experience of fruition may be hoped for. "If the spouse 'takes
care to hide himself from the wise and learned'" (Matt 11:25),
still, John of Forde affirms, "He offers himself to the little ones
to know and enjoy."[29] This enjoyment of divine love is a "kind
of happy tasting in advance of eternal glory, a transformation
into the likeness of God" (2 Cor 3:18).[30]

Gilbert of Hoyland offers advice on preparing oneself for
fruition: "Do you desire. . . to enjoy at ease the embraces of the
Bridegroom, to clasp him alone in the secret of your heart? Do
not run to open [the door] with empty hands! Action precedes
contemplation."[31] Although "it is good to pray and to long for
the Lord, to love him and hold him and enjoy him is better."[32]
Gilbert uses *frui* in several of the wordplays he delights in: "*sicut
ipsa dilecto suo vel ex voto fruitur, vel praeter votum fraudatur;*"[33]

27. OS 3; CF 32:207.

28. Epi 2.5; CF 8:80. See also Bernard, Pent 3.2; CF 53:82; OS 4.3; Luddy
3:375; Div 18.1; SBOp 6A:157; Div 25.5; SBOp 6A:191; Sent 3.45; CF 55:225; John
of Forde S 38.5; CF 43:107; S 96.7; CF 46:171.

29. S 40.5; CF 43:132-3.

30. S 71.7; CF 45:116.

31. S 43.9; CF 26:524-5.

32. S 32.8; CF 20:393.

33. "She is bereft of her beloved with greater anguish, where she could
enjoy him with greater fruitfulness." S 1.3; CF 14:46.

"alius est qui fruitur, alius qui tuetur;"[34] *"hic sponsae votum fovetur, ibi votis fruitur;"*[35] *"in sepulcro feriamur et in horto fruimur."*[36]

John of Forde sums up "all the delights with which the Bride flows" (Sg 8:5) as one delight: to enjoy the beloved."[37] "What makes [the divine] Light more loveable, most especially to be sovereignly loved," asks Isaac of Stella, "than his being givable, receivable, enjoyable [*donabilis et capabilis et fruibilis*]?"[38]

The fruition of love is described by Saint Gertrude as "that worthiest coupling of your Word and the soul which is brought about by perfect union with God."[39] She prays:

> O Love, so guard me under the shadow of your charity that after this exile when, spotless, I enter beneath your guidance into your sanctuary among the band of virgins, one small vein of your divine friendship may refresh me, and one melliflouous fruition alone may satiate me.[40]

Gertrude makes an interesting contrast between *uti* and *frui*: "To use [love] is to become intertwined in God. To enjoy [love] is to be one with God."[41]

* * *

The Cistercians are somewhat more open than Augustine to allowing for the enjoyment of other people. William of Saint-Thierry acknowledges the legitimacy of one's "enjoying both his neighbor and himself," although "he must not do so save in

34. "While one shares the joy, another stands guard." S 16.1; CF 20:204.
35. "In [the couch] the bride's desire is encouraged, in [the little bed] she enjoys its fruition." S 17.1; CF 20:218.
36. "In the tomb we have leisure; in the garden we have pleasure." S 40.5; CF 26:483.
37. S 100.6; CF 46:221.
38. S 24.17; SCh 207:110; my translation (compare CF 11:201).
39. *Spiritual Exercises*; Ex 3; CF 49:78.
40. Ex 3; CF 49:56.
41. Ex 5; CF 49:78.

[God],"[42] and Saint Bernard, writing to Rainald, abbot of Foigny, complains of "not being able to see anything of you and enjoy the comfort of your company."[43]

It is Saint Ælred, however, who speaks of this aspect of fruition at some length. He devotes a whole book to *Spiritual Friendship*, which he says,

> should be desired not for consideration of any worldly advantage or for any extrinsic cause, but from the dignity of its own nature and the feelings of the human heart, so that its fruition and reward is nothing other than itself.[44]

Interestingly, however, Ælred discusses *fruitio* not so much in this work, but in *The Mirror of Charity*. There he defines it as "possessing something with delight and joy."[45] Each one "chooses for his enjoyment what he supposes capable by its fruit of making him happy."[46] Hence the great importance of choosing well, and so he devotes a chapter to a consideration of "What We Should Choose for Enjoyment."[47] Anyone who begins to reckon himself at his proper value and to estimate the privilege of his own nature will realize that it is only God from whom we "might expect the reward of blessedness. He should be chosen by us, therefore, in preference to all else, so that we may enjoy Him."[48]

Nevertheless, since we are commanded to love (and hence to enjoy—note the difference from Augustine) both God and our neighbor,

> We should choose [not only] God that we may enjoy Him in Himself and because of Himself, [but also] our neighbor that we may enjoy him in God and God in him. For although this

42. Cant 2; CF 6:4.
43. Ep 76.1; *Letters* 106.
44. Spir amic 1.45; CF 5:60.
45. Spec car 3.8.23; CF 17:236.
46. Spec car 3.8.22; CF 17:235-6.
47. Spec car 3.25-8; CF 17:237-9.
48. Spec car 3.9.26; CF 17:238.

word enjoy is usually taken in a stricter sense—that it may be said that we should take our joy in no other thing but God alone—still, when speaking to a fellow man, Paul said "so brother, may I take my joy in you in the Lord" (Phlm 20).[49]

Later on in *The Mirror* he elaborates his views on "Those Whom We Can Enjoy in This Life":

I think it evident that at present we by no means can enjoy everyone, but only a few persons. It seems to me that we can use some people for testing, some for instruction, some for consolation, and some for sustenance. We use our enemies for testing, our teachers for instruction, our elders for consolation, and those supplying our needs for our sustenance. Only those whom we cherish with fond attachment, no matter which of these categories they may be in, do we use for sweetness of life and delight of spirit. These [persons] we can enjoy even at present, that is, we can use them with joy and delight.[50]

An interesting interplay of *uti* and *frui*. Ælred adds this advice:

Let anyone who finds it pleasant to enjoy his friend see to it that he enjoy him in the Lord, not in the world or in pleasure of the flesh, but in joyfulness of spirit. But, you ask, what does it mean to enjoy "in the Lord"? About the Lord, the apostle Paul said: "By God he has been made for us wisdom, sanctification, and justice" (1Cor 1:30). Since the Lord is wisdom, sanctification, and justice, to find enjoyment in the Lord is to find enjoyment in wisdom, sanctification, and justice. . . . in the wisdom of holy conversation, in sanctification and honor, in the justice of mutual encouragement.[51]

So in the end, the enjoyment of one's friend seems to merge into that of the Lord.

49. Spec car 3.9.28; CF 17:239.
50. Spec car 3.39.108; CF 17:297.
51. Spec car 3.40.111-2; CF 17:299-300.

* * *

Fruition is not Saint Bernard's most characteristic term for describing mystical union; he more often speaks of clinging to God, of mystical marriage, of unity of spirit. He does, however, use *fruor* and *fruitio* a number of times, and it is worthwhile to see in what ways. He warns that if the soul seeks its fruition in "things that are mortal, it clothes itself in mortality."[52] Happy is the person who can turn earthly things to his service, "using them, not enjoying them."[53] Wisdom is required to discriminate between what is to be used and what enjoyed.[54] Love, however, transcends the distinction: "it is its own fruit [*fructus ejus, usus ejus*]."[55]

The fullness of fruition, Bernard agrees with the tradition, will take place only in heaven; "when perfection is reached," in fact, "there remains nothing else to be done. There remains only to enjoy it, not to bring it about [*frui, non fieri*]."[56] There we shall indeed enjoy our God," and that

> In three different ways; for we shall see Him in all His creatures, we shall possess Him in ourselves, and—what is incomparably better and sweeter than either of these—we shall also contemplate the Trinity in itself.[57]

We shall also enjoy the presence of Mary[58] and the company of the saints.[59]

As for this life, Bernard admits that even here there may be a certain experience of *fruitio* "by those who with Mary have chosen the better part" (Luke 10:42), but its object, rather than

52. SC 82.3; CF 40:174.

53. Csi 5.2; CF 37:141; see also Sent 3.108; CF 55:225.

54. SC 50.8; CF 31:37.

55. SC 83.4; CF 40:184.

56. SC 72.2; CF 40:64.

57. OS 4.3; Luddy 3:388. "The Trinity alone enjoys itself [*sola se fruitur*]" 1 Nov 4; Luddy 2:361.

58. Assp 1.1; Luddy 3:219.

59. OS 5.5; Luddy 3:388.

God, is freedom of pleasure [*complaciti liberate*].[60] Our main occupation here below, however, is to "learn from our freedom of counsel not to abuse free choice, in order that one day we may be able fully to enjoy freedom of pleasure."[61]

In his early Sermons on the Canticle, Bernard uses *fruitio* in an ecclesial sense:

> Only the Church of the perfect [reclines within] during the present time. We too, however, have grounds for hope. Imperfect though we be, let us rest outside the doors, rejoicing in hope (Rm 12;12). Meantime the bride and groom are within, enjoying the mystery of their mutual embraces.[62]

Yet each soul which has become a bride can also aspire to fruition, "enjoying the delight of the Bride-groom's visit" in its own special place.[63]

It is not until sermon eighty-five of the Canticle that Bernard elaborates on *fruitio* as a mystical experience attainable in this life. He begins by giving seven reasons that the soul seeks the Word; the last, and most sublime, is "that she may enjoy Him."[64] Later in the sermon he attempts a description of this enjoyment:

> In [the soul's] awareness of the Word she is not aware of herself. This happens when the mind is enraptured by the unutterable sweetness of the Word, so that it withdraws, or rather is transported, and escapes from itself to enjoy the Word.

This experience is on a higher plane than even that of apostolic fruitfulness:

60. Gra 15; CF 19:71.

61. Gra 24; CF 19:83.

62. SC 14.5; CF 4:101; see also SC 61.2; CF 31:141; SC 76.1; CF 40:110. With respect to "*fruamur cupitis amplexibus:*" with its reminiscence of Prov 7:18, the *Dictionnaire de Spiritualité* (5:1554) remarks on Bernard's familiar, almost playful use of Scripture, whereby "the prostitute's invitation is transposed into the mystical embrace of the Bridegroom and the Bride," Christ and the Church.

63. SC 23.9; CF 7:34; see also SC 51.6; CF 31:41.

64. SC 85.1; CF 40:196.

> The soul is affected in one way when it is made fruitful by
> the Word, in another when it enjoys the Word [*fructificans,*
> *fruens*]. . . . A mother is happy in her child; a bride is even
> happier in her bridegroom's embrace. . . . That is what I
> spoke of before, when I said that the final reason for the soul
> to seek the Word was to enjoy Him in bliss.[65]

Bernard forestalls further explanation by continuing:

> There may be someone who will go on to ask me, "What
> does it mean to enjoy the Word?" I would answer that he
> must find someone who has experience of it, and ask him.
> Do you suppose, if I were granted that experience that I
> could ever describe to you what is beyond description? . . .
> Whoever is curious to know what it means to enjoy the
> Word, make ready your mind, not your ear! The tongue
> does not teach this, grace does.[66]

* * *

It may be that this sermon shows the influence of Bernard's
great friend, William of Saint-Thierry, who speaks much more
frequently of *fruitio* and gives a rich development to the concept.
Fruitio and *fruor* run like a refrain through his *Commentary on the
Song of Songs*, expressing not only the goal of all the soul's striv-
ing, but the very reason for its creation: "O Lord our God, you
created us to your image and likeness, it is plain, that we might
contemplate you and have fruition of you."[67]

This goal is true in a special way for monastics, as William
tells the monks of Mont-Dieu:

> It is for others to serve God, it is for you to cling to him; it
> is for others to believe in God, know him, love him and

65. SC 85.13; CF 40:209-10.
66. SC 85.14; CF 40:210.
67. Cant 1; CF 6:3.

revere him; it is for you to taste him, understand him, be acquainted with him, enjoy him.[68]

Since we can only find our true fruition in God, it is a great disorder if we attempt to find it in creatures:

> When we love any creature, not to use [*uti*] it for you but to enjoy it in itself, love becomes not love but greed or lust or something of the kind, losing with the loss of freedom even the grace of the name of love. Man's whole sin consists in enjoying amiss and using amiss [*male frui et male usi*].[69]

Further on in his *Commentary*, William expands on what he said in the Prologue:

> Man was created to the image of God for this purpose, that devoutly mindful of God in order to understand him, humbly understanding him in order to love him and loving him with ardor and wisdom until he attains to possession and fruition [*fruendi affectum*] of him, he might be a rational animal.[70]

"By loving [God] to enjoy Him and delight in Him is proper to human reason in its perfection."[71]

The fruition that William speaks of is an experience that one can aspire to even on earth. Although fruition "properly belongs to the perfect," it is sometimes granted to the less perfect.[72] It is more often, however, experienced by the mature soul that has advanced in the stages that William enumerates: "First, the will moves the soul toward God, then love carries her forward, charity contemplates, and wisdom enjoys."[73]

---

68. Ep frat 16; CF 12:14. See Gilbert S 32.8; CF 20:393: "It is good to pray and to long for the Lord, but to love him and hold him and enjoy him is better."

69. Cant 2; CF 6:4. See also Cant 99; CF 6:161.

70. Cant 88; CF 6:73.

71. Cant 89; CF 6:73.

72. Ep frat 191; CF 12:76.

73. Nat am 2; CF 30:88.

At times, William contrasts the anxiety caused by God's absence with the fruition of his presence,[74] or the labor of understanding with the joy of fruition.[75] But more frequently—in this matter following Augustine—the contrast is between desire and fruition:

> The love of him who desires is not the same as the love of him who has fruition. The love of desire burns even in the darkness but gives no light; whereas the love of him who has fruition is wholly in the light, because fruition itself is the light of the lover.[76]

Desire and fruition might seem to be mutually exclusive, but William sees them rather as "harmonious antitheses."[77] Fruition is the "reward for immense desire."[78] "Desiring love is sometimes rewarded with sight; the reward of sight is delight [*fruitionem*] and delight earns the perfecting of love."[79] Hence William prays: "Enlighten and quicken the desire of him who tends toward you, that it may become the love of one having fruition of you."[80] The place of fruition is charity itself, "the heart which . . . is solitary in God."[81]

The capacity for fruition increases as the soul recovers its likeness to God; this principle is basic for William, "No one who contemplates you," he addresses God, "reaches fruition of You save insofar as he becomes like to you."[82] "The degree of fruition becomes the degree of progress which accompanies it, and there can be no fruition apart from the likeness which brings it about."[83]

---

74. Cant 76; CF 6:63-4. "Because understanding lacked its light, love was unable to find its joy in fruition."
75. Cant 115; CF 6:93.
76. Cant 60; CF 6:48.
77. Cant 120; CF 6:97.
78. Cant 67; CF 6:54.
79. Cont 5; CF 3:43.
80. Cant 4; CF 6:6-7.
81. Cant 4; CF 6:6-7.
82. Cant 1; CF 6:3.
83. Cant 94; CF 6:76. See also Ep frat 30; CF 12:19-20.

Christ therefore advises the soul: "If you aspire to the fullness of fruition, labor and strive to possess the fullness of my likeness."[84]

William goes on to speak of the

> mutual resemblance in beauty and mutual fruition which draw [the Bridegroom and bride} together. For it is not only that we have fruition of God; God himself so enjoys our goodness, insofar as he delights in it and deigns to find it pleasing.[85]

So did God delight in his creation, according to the first chapter of Genesis.

This "wonderful union and mutual fruition" between humanity and God, the created spirit and the Uncreated, the Bride and the Bridegroom, "is nothing else than the unity of the Father and the Son"—indeed, the Holy Spirit himself, "God, Charity, at once Giver and Gift."[86] In fact, the Holy Spirit is both the One who "teaches how to find [God], possess Him and enjoy Him" and "the gladness of him who enjoys."[87]

Any fruition we may experience on earth, however, is momentary and inchoative, leading us only to greater longing for "the day that remains forever in the noontide of warmth and light, wisdom and understanding, love and blessed fruition"[88] in heaven, which will be

> the full kiss and the full embrace, the power of which is the wisdom of God, its sweetness, the Holy Spirit; and its perfection, the full fruition of the Divinity [*perfectio plena fruition divinitas*], and God all in all.[89]

This, after all, is the goal of the journey.

84. Cant 107; CF 6:87.
85. Cant 94; CF 6:76. See also Ep frat 30; CF 12:19-20.
86. Cant 95; CF 6:77-8.
87. Ep frat 266; CF 12:96.
88. Cant 56; CF 6:45.
89. Cant 132; CF 6:107.